IT'S BEEN A **LONG TIME** COMING...

NOMUSA XABA IS A GIFTED and sensitive storyteller. She brings this storytelling prowess to her writings. With careful prose and striking poetry her book reads like listening to her. She allows us to be with her as she tells of this important historical transition. You become immersed in the story and without realizing it you have become a part of her story. You can't stop listening. You can't stop reading.

—*Tejumola F. Ologboni*

STORYTELLER AND FORMER BOARD MEMBER
NATIONAL ASSOCIATION OF BLACK STORYTELLERS

MY PARENTS, RICHARD AND Armelia Packard, at a New Year's Eve party, 1954.

IT'S BEEN A **LONG TIME** COMING...

A MEMOIR BY Nomusa Xaba

MILWAUKEE, WISCONSIN

CONTENTS

CHAPTER 9

CHAPTER 10

CHAPTER 11

CHAPTER 12

CHAPTER 13

CHAPTER 14

CHAPTER 15

CHAPTER 16

CHAPTER 17

THE POEMS

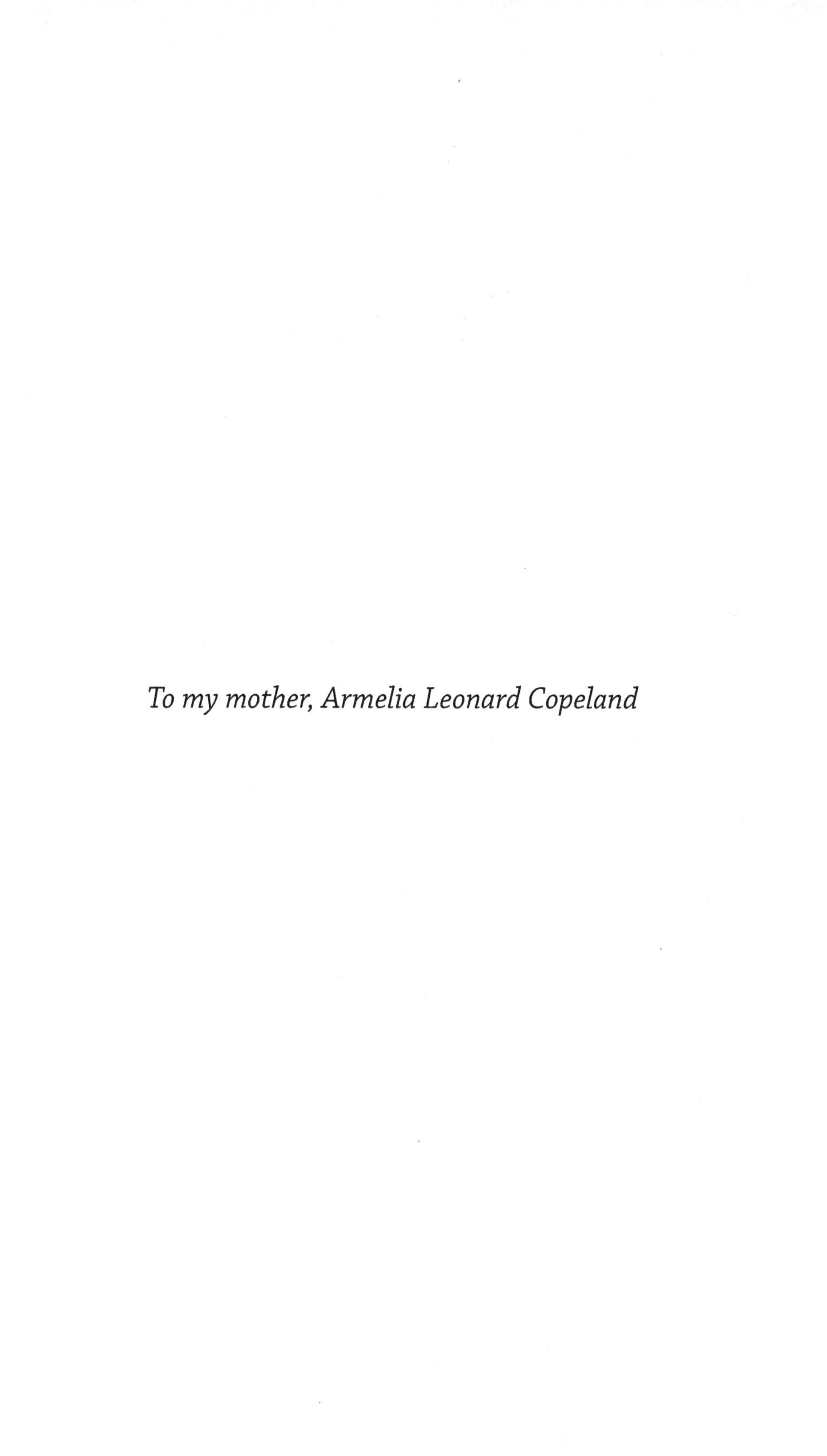

To my mother, Armelia Leonard Copeland

FIRST EDITION

ISBN-13 978-0-615-30730-5
ISBN-10 0-615-30730-2
Library of Congress Control Number: 9780615307305

Cover: the author at two years old Chicago, 1948.

Design by Cheryl Hanna
IMAGES & ILLUMINATIONS

Clearwater Publishing

CLEARWATER PUBLISHING
c/o Genhi Bailey
PO Box 811021
Los Angeles, CA 90081
414-460-8285
mamanomusa@gmail.com

PREFACE

WHEN THINKING OF A preface for this book, I was reminded of two things. One was a billboard picture of a ninety-five-year-old college graduate. They say a picture is worth a thousand words, and just the picture with the caption, "ninety-five-year-old woman oldest graduate" spoke volumes. If she could have the sheer guts to finish school at her age, then any excuses the rest of us might have pale by comparison. The other was a popular story of the elderly woman who always wanted to get her degree but life got in the way. Her chance finally came, but her children protested, saying "Why do you want to go to school, Mom, by the time you finish you'll be seventy-five!" Her reply was "Yes, I'll be seventy-five with a degree!" These examples resonate with my feeling that no matter how long it takes, your dreams can come true.

The concept for this book started in 1970, and here it is almost forty years later, finally manifest! During that time the format has changed many times, as it now stands, it is an autobiographical memoir complete with poetry and pictures... a snippet of my life, as though someone was following me, pointing out some of the highlights... only that someone is me! As a card-carrying artist and educator, I now make my living as a storyteller and educational consultant. This book is an opportunity for you, the reader, to see into the inner workings of what has brought me to this point in my life, so that you too can be inspired to take that next step in your own life. Dare to write your own book or whatever it is that is burning in your heart. Commit to doing it no matter how long it takes! Remember you have all the support you need, just take the time to see it beginning, and give your heart a chance to express itself with clarity and honesty. I am grateful for this opportunity to present this labor of love and I hope it serves as an encouragement to you and others who have dreams that seem to take a long time in coming...

ACKNOWLEDGMENTS

SHWABADA, NONKOSI! I HUMBLY thank all of my ancestors who paved the way for me. My thanks to my father and stepmother, Richard L. and Anita Packard. Thanks to all of my children Genhi, Maqhawe, Makhosi, Sipho, and Dingane; and grandchildren Paris, Armani, Sizwe and Lindiwe. Special thanks to my spiritual sons: Zondizitha Sanjari for his unwavering, continued and unbiased support over many years and Themba Khumalo for speaking in a quiet, forceful way.

A sincere thanks to Aisha Lumumba for her encouragement. And last but not least, thanks to my aunt and uncle, Sylvia Gwendolyn and Willie Rowe, for standing with me and supporting me through every phase of my life.

IT'S BEEN A **LONG TIME** COMING...

SITTING, LEFT TO RIGHT: Auntie (Henrietta Turner, my maternal great aunt), Grandma (Louise Parker, my maternal great grandmother) Mu' Dear (Elmira Leonard, my maternal grandmother), Gwen (Sylvia Gwendolyn Leonard, my maternal aunt), Daddy (Howard Leonard, my maternal grandfather), Mama (Armelia M. Leonard Packard, my mother). Standing left, Uncle Horace (Horace Ford Leonard, my maternal uncle), and standing right is Dad (Richard L. Packard, my father).

CHAPTER I

THE HOUSE THAT MU' DEAR AND DADDY BUILT

THIS HISTORIC PICTURE WAS taken on the fortieth birthday of my maternal grandmother, Elmira Leonard, February 18, 1945, at the family house located at 13610 Turner Avenue, Robbins, Illinois. My grandmother, a visionary entrepreneur and the rock of the family, was always affectionately known as Mu' Dear (short for Mother Dear) by the family. Mu' Dear died a few short months after this picture was taken, and a year before my birth. So what was originally intended as a family picture, honoring her birth, became a monument to family love. In our family, the picture will continue to be cherished by many generations to come. The family house where the picture was taken served as a refuge for everyone in our family. It holds many stories. Everyone in that picture at some point lived in that house and it housed my earliest memories of being alive.

CHAPTER 2

FRIDAY

MY IMMEDIATE FAMILY, MY parents, my older brother and I, moved into the family house at 13610 Turner Avenue when I was a baby. Already in residence were my grandfather (always known as Daddy to me), my Aunt Gwen (five years my senior), and my great aunt Henrietta Turner (always called Auntie). Auntie had moved in to take care of Gwen who was only four years old when her mother died. She had no children of her own and her husband had died many years before. She was a kind soul who masked her true feelings quite well. She rarely directly challenged my outspoken great grandmother, but she shielded herself quite well, by keeping a very sober face and staying out of harm's way. Not an easy task when dealing with a younger sister who was by anyone's measurement, a drama queen.

Auntie didn't talk much, but what she had to say carried weight and she always treated us children as though we were very special. She was a quiet but powerful woman. The house was alive with energy, people, and music. I basked in the music of Paul Robeson, the Five Blind Boys, Jimmy Lunceford, Count Basie, and Mahalia Jackson to name a few. Music was the fabric of our life and I soaked it all in.

But my immediate family's move out of the secure web of love the family house provided came too soon for me. It was at this critical time in my young life that I felt the powerful shift from, *all of us together* in the same house, to *all of us together* but in different houses. I was four years old, not yet ready for kindergarten, when my parents got an apartment on Chicago's west side. It was spring, the middle of the school year. Since my brother Ricky was in first grade and in school in Robbins and since my parents didn't want to split us up, they decided the best thing for the family was for them to live and work in Chicago during the week and visit us on the weekends. We were left in the expert care of the "Big Mommas," my great grandmother and her sister, Auntie.

I remember that Sunday evening when my parents left for the big city, everyone, the adults and all the children were hovering in the living room in anticipation of this historic event. I remember my parents standing at the door, but instead of them leaving they hesitated to look at me once more. Since I was the youngest of the three children and didn't quite understand the full impact of what was going on, everyone was keen to give me lots of assurance that my parents would be back, that it was the best thing for everyone and that I would be all right. But at this crucial moment of departure their assurances were not working. I still had a lot of questions but I didn't quite have the words to express my doubts and fears. I was not at all convinced that I would ever see them again. I needed some answers; and there my parents stood in the doorway, anxious but determined not to go until their little girl was okay with this.

This was the moment of truth. Everyone was looking at me, I was so young, what words could I use to express my fears? I knew I had to speak clearly now if I were to get any answers. So I insisted again on knowing when they would be back. That seemed reasonable; everyone said they would be back, but when? In unison all the adults seemingly relieved said, *Friday*. "Friday, what is that?" I blurted out.

They all seemed to know what it was and when it was, but I didn't. I couldn't trust something as dear as my parents to something I couldn't understand, like Friday. My four-year-old mind tried to wrap itself around that foreign concept. Friday? In my world, every day was just like the other, all filled with blissful play. What was Friday? Sensing my ambivalence, Auntie, always ready to rescue in time of need, stepped in and assured me she would teach me the days of the week and I would see that on Friday my parents would come back. Well, that calmed my fears enough for them to leave.

I stayed as close to Auntie as I could. Every day upon awakening I asked her the inevitable question. "What day is today?" Every day she would tell me, and then I would quickly ask the next obvious question, "how many days until Friday?" This little game eased my concerns about my parents coming back, gave me something to focus on besides missing them, and helped me to gain confidence in the elders in my life.

Finally I woke up one day and was told it was Friday! But where were the parents? I guess I expected for them to just magically appear. Doubt started to seep in. I wanted to believe Auntie but I had no proof. Everyone said they would be back on Friday, today was Friday, so where were the parents? Then Auntie said it's not time yet. Time? What's time? I was told they would be back at evening time, after breakfast, lunch, and supper but before bedtime... and then, like a miracle, they both walked through the door at evening time, after breakfast, lunch, and supper but before bedtime!

That first gruesome week helped me to get through the others and I eventually got to know the days of the week and how they followed each other. This was getting to be fun, everyone had told me the truth and it really was all right! Whenever I got lonesome for my parents, I just counted the days of the week. I got pretty good at naming the days of the week. Having mastered that, I moved on to telling time. It started as I watched for my grandfather to come home from work in the evening. He left every day before breakfast and returned after lunch but before supper! I could anticipate his arrival by just paying attention and after awhile I could tell when to stop playing and begin the watch.

I would sit in the window and watch for him. Before long I would spot him just as he turned the corner from 137th Street and came down Turner Avenue. That was our signal (mine and the dog's) to fly down the road to meet him. Jumping into his anxious arms like that everyday, Daddy and I became great friends . . . such great friends in fact that we developed our own Saturday morning ritual, repeated every Saturday for I don't know how long . . .

CHAPTER 3

OL' MAN RIVER

SATURDAY MORNING, THE house is clean, everyone has gone shopping...I'm dressed like a princess is dressed on Saturday, pretty but not overdone...no one is around...no one except my grandfather and me...and the signal for the ritual to begin is my Uncle Skeeter's weekly Saturday morning arrival at the family house. Lights, Camera, Action...the show is about to begin. Uncle Skeeter has arrived, so Daddy (my grandfather) carefully places me on the newly polished dining room table while he and Uncle Skeeter comfortably settle down on the couch facing me anticipating the "Show of Shows." Then Daddy gives the command "SANG GAL!" and I start to sing my passionate version of "Ol' Man River." I stop midway through the song and look at them as they nod their heads, and their eyes approvingly say, "Go ahead, sing the rest of the song." By now I'm trying to put some emotion and movement into the song and sing it the way I heard Paul Robeson do it. They applaud...I curtsy...and pridefully, as though he is holding a precious cargo, Daddy picks me up off that table, turns to look at Uncle Skeeter and says, "I don't know what that gal's gonna be but she...*GONNA BE SOMETHING.*"

CHAPTER 4

DANCING WITH MY FATHER

THE FOLLOWING PICTURE, TAKEN September 27, 1953, was on the occasion of the wedding of Alline Rutland and Willie Carter at the New Zion Church on 14th and Woods in Chicago, Illinois.

My dad had practiced with me for some months before the wedding. We were dance partners and this was to be my big debut, except I didn't know it! In those days when people got married, they hired a live band (usually a trio) to play at their house. I had never seen a live band before, so it was a special moment for me.

The energy was joyful, excited, and when the band started to play, everyone started to dance, including my dad and I. I remembered all the steps he taught me and kept up with the fast pace, but it was when my dad let my hand go, (a signal to improvise) that everyone moved off the floor as my dad and I stole the show!

FROM LEFT TO RIGHT: adults Rudolph Ashford, Hattie Palmer, Elmer Carter, Willie Carter, Alline Rutland, Anna Mae Redmond, and William Reed; children Dwight Martin, and the author, Patricia Packard (Nomusa Xaba).

CHAPTER 5

ROCKWELL 2-4557

A life narrative told in the precocious voice of a seven–year-old.

YOU WANNA KNOW WHAT my phone number is? My phone number is Ro 2-4557 and I live at 1832 West Washburn on the west side of Chicago, Illinois. *And my dad?* My dad, he a glass man. My dad, he makes glass at the Dearborn Glass Company. The Dearborn Glass Company is very far away. My dad, he have to get up real early to get to the Dearborn Glass Company. I know 'cause every morning I try to get up before my dad leaves, but every day he's gone before I can get up! But my dad for real he a jazz man! On the week-ends my dad he play the jazz music on his trumpet. Friday night is special, on Friday night me and my dad we be dance partners and he teach me all the fancy steps. My dad he play music on the record player so loud everybody in the neighborhood can hear. My dad say jazz is our music, the music of the colored people. He say it's the best music in the world!

And my mamma? My mamma she works at the Cook County Hospital for the colored people. And sometime, I get to go to my mamma's job and I get to wait for my mamma in the big lobby that has the big water fountain! It's so big you can just sit on the edge and watch the water, sometimes people throw pennies into it, to make they wish come true. My mamma say she always wanted to be a nurse but they wouldn't let her on account of she had rheumatic fever when she was little and it left her with the rheumatic heart. So she became a nurse's aide instead. But she say that don't make no sense to her, 'cause nurse's aides work a lot harder than nurses!

My mamma she can't dance too fast on account of the rheumatic heart she got, so that's why my dad always have me be his dance partner, he say she too slow. But she say that's alright with her, she just dance in the corner by herself and "do her number."

And my great grandmamma? My great grandmamma sometimes she take me for walks in the neighborhood and my great grandmamma she knows everybody. And always always when she take me for a walk somebody stop us and they always say, "Mrs. Parker, whose little girl is that? Who little girl that is?" And she always proudly says, why this is my great grandbaby and then they always say "Oh, why you must be Mrs. Leonard's grandbaby. You had a wonderful grandmother, *she used to do my hair*. Why she was the first colored beautician on the Westside." And then they look sadly up in the sky like they seeing an angel or something and say "Sho is a shame the way she died, so sudden."

I hear this story over and over, pretty soon I get to know what they gonna say before they say it! But what I don't know is "how did she die so sudden." So, I started listening to the grown people when they be talking, when I wasn't supposed to be listening. And the story goes kinda like this... see my grandmamma (Mu'Dear) took sick one day, she had stomach problems, all the neighbors came and everybody tried to help her but it was no use, she got worse and worse. So my granddaddy had to rush her to the Cook County Hospital for the colored people. But you see, they lived in Robbins and the County was on the Westside and that was at least forty-five minutes away. He passed by a lot of other hospitals on the way, but they didn't take colored people. He wanted to stop at the other hospitals, people always asked him why he didn't stop and he always say, wasn't no use stopping if they wouldn't take her, it'd just waste time and this was an emergency. Anyway as the story goes, he got her to the hospital but she died a few hours later... *but me?*

I'm just a kid and I love to play and my favorite game is HIDE AND GO SEEK... and whoever is *It,* covers up his eyes, puts his head to the tree and sings:

Last Night
Night before
24 robbers at my door
I got up to let them in

Hit them in the head

With a rolling pin

ALL HID?

And you must be HID before he gets to the end of the song...

So one Saturday we were playing HIDE AND GO SEEK and my dad was sitting in the car talking to one of his friends and I was looking for a good place to hide... and I discovered a secret place that nobody had ever found before! It was in the street on the side of the car in front of my dad's... nobody had ever hid there before!

But before It got to the end of the song, my dad ordered me to go upstairs! I went but when I got to the stoop I turned around and asked my dad, why? He said I was going to get a whooping! I cried all the way up the stairs and when I reached the top my momma asked me to stop crying and tell her what was wrong. When I told her my tale of woe, she opened the window and hollered out at my dad to ask him why was I being sent upstairs to get a whooping when all I had been doing was playing outside... and he said, "I know what she was doing, I've been sitting here in this car watching her play. And if I've told her once, I've told her a thousand times, DON'T PLAY IN THE STREET..."

Well, despite my wails, he came upstairs and he gave me that whooping. But from that day to this, I've never played in the street ever again...

Last Night

Night before

24 robbers at my door

I got up to let them in

Hit them in the head

With a rolling pin

ALL HID?

MY DAD, AT SEVENTY-FIVE years old, with his trumpet.

SONG FOR MY FATHER

Written on the occasion of my father's sixtieth birthday, March 25, 1982. These were some of the songs that were played every Friday night that my father used to teach me to dance.

I am the One-O'Clock Jump [1]
Stompin' at the Savoy[2]
and even April in Paris[3]
Duke Ellington's child
heir to the throne
heritage passed from mouth to mouth

hand to hand
rhythm to rhythm
is Duke Ellington
Continuing on and on . . .

Hear Charlie Parker . . . blow
Bo . . . Diddley
Howlin' Wolf . . . Howl
for us to remember
we are children
of long ago—NOW
old moans from a church

told to us was

long ago—"come before times."

way back times—NOW

flow rhythms flow

through me and to the next

One O'Clock Jump

Stompin' at the Savoy

and even

April in Paris

1. "One O'Clock Jump" (song popularized by the Count Basie Orchestra).
2. "April in Paris" (a 1932 song that was a 1956 hit for Count Basie and his orchestra.)
3. "Stompin' at the Savoy" (song popularized in 1935 by the Chick Webb and Benny Goodman Orchestras; it was recorded by the Duke Ellington Orchestra, for Capitol records, in 1955.)

CHAPTER 6

THE DAY THAT DADDY DIED

THE TENSION WAS VERY thick in both the Robbins family house and our house on the Westside. My maternal grandfather (Daddy) was very sick. My step-grandmother, Miss Tina, and my mother were in a bitter dispute over the care that he should receive.

Miss Tina believed in the power of prayer as the ultimate and only cure and chose to pray nonstop around the bed of my then very-sick grandfather. The saints from the church came too and they managed to keep a twenty-four hour vigil, so no matter what time I tried to sneak in to see him there was some adult there to block me. During those critical days of his illness, I was not allowed near him or his room. No one seemed to understand that he was my friend and that we needed to be together, he might feel better if he could see me.

My grandfather was dying and all I could do was to try and be close to his bedroom door, before one of the saints or a family member would shoo me away. Ultimate feelings of helplessness overcame me. As my loved ones hotly debated (argued) over the right course of treatment for my much ailing grandfather, I watched and wondered who was right, and if my grandfather would ever get better. He was so afraid of hospitals, especially Cook County Hospital (commonly know as the "The County") that was the usual one used for people of color. Isn't that the same place he had driven his wife to eight short years before, angrily bypassing so many "white" hospitals? Isn't it the last place he had seen her alive? Isn't that the same place where they had killed his wife?

He could never say it out loud, but he thought it. Thoughts are things and I could hear him loudly thinking. "Don't take me to that place, I don't want to go to that place, it is the place where you die."

My grandfather, a short man with a warm look on his face and a brown-red skin tone, was succumbing to the ravages of death. He was afraid and I, his friend and granddaughter, could not help him. The bitter family disagreement over his treatment expanded and the adults started taking sides, meanwhile the saints of the church held forth, around the clock, at his bedside. Finally, at my mother's ultimate insistence, my grandfather was transferred to the County after having confessed Christ on his sick bed.

On March 5, 1954, the family car showed up to pick my brother and me up from school. And the *whole family* was in the family car. They motioned for us to get in. The air was silent, thick, somber... this could not be good, no one had ever picked us up from school before.

I was waiting for someone in the car to say something, give me the news, why were they here, what was going on, but there was a deep quietude. It was finally broken by talk of funeral arrangements. I was immediately angry that no one had the courtesy to tell me directly that my grandfather had died. I sensed that might be the case when they picked us up. But why didn't they just say so? Children just don't get the respect!

Somberly, I tried to understand this thing called death. Daddy had died; this was the day Daddy died...what did it mean to die? Would his spirit come to me and talk to me the way Miss Tina said spirits come to her? Or would there just be a big void in my life and I would just miss him forever? I was consoled by the memories that started to flood my mind...memories of those great days we had together when I was four, calculating the exact time for him to come home from work. Watching out the front porch window for him to come and me and the dog running down the steps, down the road and jumping into his welcome arms...Daddy was home! Memories of the secret ritual he and I and Uncle Skeeter had every Saturday morning, memories of his now infamous words, now ringing in my ears, "I don't know what that gal's gonna be, but she *gonna be something*!" Through all the tears, I knew it would be okay. You can't take away memories. He believed in me, so all I had to do was believe in myself and I would have my Daddy forever!

MY GREAT UNCLE SOL and his wife, Rebecca Street, taken in the 1920s.

CHAPTER 9

THE DAY FREEDOM WOULD COME

WAS IN JAIL 3 days…

Or was it 3 years?

Could have been 300 years

The way it felt

It was a concrete jail

Concrete floors

Concrete walls

A big concrete door

And inside that concrete door

A metal door

Locked, with me inside

Once the doors closed

First the metal

Then the concrete

Every second seemed magnified...I was eighteen years old and in Greenville, Mississippi, the "Pearl of the Delta." Greenville was a small Southern town that prided itself on being different from the violent reputation Mississippi is infamous for. It was proud of its reputation for being "liberal" on race issues. I was a Freedom Fighter, a civil rights worker for CORE (The Congress of Racial Equality). I was straight from the big city of Chicago, a newcomer to Mississippi; new to the red clay dirt, new to the plantations that looked like they hadn't changed since the Civil War except fewer people were left on them, new to people making forty dollars a month for back-breaking work, new to the fear of singing freedom songs too loud lest the white folks who owned the plantation you lived on heard you.

My great-grandmother, Mrs. Louise Parker, had fled the Mississippi Delta abruptly at the turn of the twentieth century after she intervened for her brother who was about to be lynched by a mob of angry whites. The story, as I heard it, was a dispute with a white man over a chicken. In those days whites could just come on the property of any black person and take what they wanted. It was called racial courtesy! Anyway, while my Great-Uncle Sol was away, a white neighbor came on his property and took a chicken. When Uncle Sol heard what happened, he got his shotgun and went over to the man's house and took his chicken back. Before he could get back home with the now-disputed chicken, the white man and his neighbors arrived, disarmed my uncle, tied him to the back of a truck and dragged him to town. Once in town they made their case to the local townspeople. A crowd quickly formed and Uncle Sol was tied to a tree and about to be lynched. My alarmed great-grandmother, determined not to let her brother be lynched, ran to an influential white man she had done some work for to beg for his intervention. His influence managed to stop the mob, for now. But my uncle was now a marked man, and he had to leave the Delta that night. Traumatized and bruised, but happy to be alive, Uncle Sol had to leave his family including his wife and six children, his property, everything, and flee first to Memphis, then St. Louis and finally to Chicago to save his life. His extended family including my great-grandmother fled very quickly thereafter. It was dangerous in those parts to be the relative of an "uppity nigger," someone who would dare to stand up for their basic rights.

So here I was in 1965 the great-grandchild of these "uppity niggers" back in the Mississippi Delta. At our first family meeting on the subject of my going to Mississippi, I was still a high school student. My brother and I called a family meeting and he agreed to be my "lawyer." Being the "lawyer" for your sibling was a family tradition my brother and I devised to help each other. When we were in serious trouble, we would agree to speak on the other's behalf. We all gathered in the living room. Everyone was noticeably tense. My brother did a great job as my lawyer, I thought. He outlined my dedication to the civil rights movement, my good grades, and my responsible behavior—all with great articulation. All was going well until he said he was asking for permission on my behalf to go to Mississippi

THE AUTHOR WITH JAMES Farmer (National Director of CORE) in 1964 in Chicago.

for what was being billed as Mississippi Freedom Summer 1964. My parents thought I had lost my mind; their reaction was swift, my father first screamed a pledge that he would kill me himself before letting a "cracker" kill me; my mother sobbed uncontrollably. The meeting was over. I was seventeen when we had this initial family "meeting." But here we were six months later; I was eighteen, had graduated from high school, and was working full time as a community organizer and managing the Westside office of CORE. I had my own apartment with three other female civil rights workers. This all seemed to give my family enough time to work it through and to give their blessings. It was December 1964, Freedom Summer was over; it was my time to go to Mississippi.

I took a break from the intensity of work in Chicago and went to Milwaukee for a week to relax before going to Mississippi. The plan was for my family to meet me at the train station in Chicago and see me off. At Union Station in Chicago, only my father and brother were at the station, my mother was noticeably absent. When my flashing eyes asked "Where's Mom?" my dad quickly informed me that my mother became ill enough to be taken to the hospital that morning, no diagnosis yet, all we knew was that she couldn't walk. My dad had to carry her down three flights of stairs. That was all I needed to hear, the plan was off. I was going to the hospital! It was my father's insistence that I get on the train but mostly his message to me from my mother that turned the tide. From her hospital bed she had instructed him to *"put her on the train."* Even though my parents disagreed and worried for my safety; they respected my choice. It became a sort of "right of passage" for me and my very wise parents didn't want to thwart my growth. My father and brother put me on the train and to console myself I promised to write my mother every day.

So off we went, Peggy, my best friend, and I. At our tender age we were already veteran civil rights workers. We had undergone vigorous training in both community organization and non-violent demonstration techniques. We had helped to organize many demonstrations, including the now famous March on Washington and worked as community organizers on the Westside of Chicago, walking the streets during periods of heightened tensions between the community and police, and we had helped to quell more than one potential riot. We had gone to jail in Chicago and come across the notoriously brutal Chicago police on too many occasions. We were unashamedly young, idealistic and out to change the world—today. But our experiences were in Chicago. Now, here we were in Mississippi and we really didn't know what to expect. Mississippi Freedom Summer 1964 had yielded three civil rights workers brutalized and killed in Philadelphia, Mississippi; the thought of it was always sobering. It sort of hung in the air and never really left you. This was only December 1964, could that happen to us? Should we abandon these plans? The trip by train had itself been uneventful, quite a needed juxtaposition from the intensity of the previous months, and of the months to come.

To our dismay, upon our arrival in Mississippi, Peggy and I had been split up; she sent to work in Greenville and I was sent many miles away to Rankin County. What followed was a reunion of sorts, because we had been separated for several months. I had come to Greenville to learn a phonics based literacy program from Peggy. She had just learned it from another civil rights worker in her area and we thought it would fit right in for me in Rankin County with my newfound students. I had started to teach Mrs. Laura Evans and her daughter and anyone else who wanted to learn to read in Rankin County. But I was going off the top of my head, I had never taught reading before and felt I needed some guidelines and some training.

Peggy and I agreed that it would be worth my while to spend a week in Greenville to learn it. The phonics-based program was wonderful and worked very quickly with eager-to-learn adults. We had maybe two hands-on sessions; I remember it being a very gratifying experience to teach seventy-year-old farm workers how to read for the first time in their lives. But nostalgia was short lived; there were other pressing social issues...

I can't even remember what the issue was; all I know is that a coalition of organizations in Greenville decided to organize a demonstration. CORE, our organization, was part of the coalition and we worked for CORE, so we switched from teaching literacy to making picket signs in a flash. It all seemed like a whirlwind. Staying up all night printing clever slogans on picket signs made by hand, rehearsing the demonstration route and what position to take to protect our vital organs if police became violent and started to beat us, renewing our pledge to non-violence, rehearsing freedom songs, etc. Before I knew it, we were picketing. That was an illegal act and we expected to be arrested. Decisions were made that we should to pack the jail and not allow ourselves to be released until our demands were met. The demonstrations were on, we sang nonstop, one freedom song after another, energy was high. Then the police chief came with the big paddy wagon. He asked us to leave; we continued to sing...one by one he asked us to leave, one by one we refused and one by one we got into the paddy wagon. Greenville lived up to its reputation; everything was so orderly, almost as if we were acting out a play. There was no violence, no disrespect on either side. We were not handcuffed. It was quite a contrast from the violent behavior we had witnessed and experienced by the Chicago police. Maybe twenty to thirty people filled that paddy wagon and they had more lined up. All in all, I think we had a hundred people go to jail that day. There were no disrespectful strip searches. There were about thirty of us women in one huge cell with bunk beds and one open toilet. We had no contact with our leaders. After about a day people started being bailed out (bail was always organized before the demonstration so people could estimate how long they would be in jail.) But this one was supposed to be a big one; we were to stay in indefinitely, until all our demands were met. We were all quite confused. This was the demonstration of demonstrations, this would be the day freedom would come. How could we be bailed out and freedom was not here?

My youthful mind could not wrap itself around this concept. Weren't we selling out to the establishment by leaving? So I decided that I would stay in jail; the others could leave if they chose but I would stay until freedom came. I convinced another girl to stay with me, she was younger than I and we vowed not to leave each other in this cold, sterile, depressing environment. When it was our turn, we would leave victoriously together. One by one people started to go. The police spent a few days trying to get us to leave but we stubbornly refused. What an unusual turn of circumstances, prisoners who refused to *leave* on moral grounds! Finally they had to send in our lawyer who explained that tactics had changed, there was a rally being planned for that night and everyone was waiting for us. My bond had been paid and my leaders had ordered me to leave. I tried to get them to take my young friend first; knowing she would be afraid all alone. The lawyer assured me it was okay. It was just the paperwork, just the logistics; she would be out within the hour. Reluctantly, I left the jail, hugging my friend and reminding the lawyer of the promise to release her ASAP. I was taken immediately to the rally that had hundreds of people in attendance; I was relieved to see my young friend arrive moments after me. We were heralded as heroes; people hugged us and shook our hands. A mixture of emotions overtook me. I was overwhelmed, dismayed, stunned, and confused all at once. But I wondered if this was the *day that freedom would come*…

COMING OF AGE. THE author at thirteen years old at a friend's house in Chicago.

THE AUTHOR (AT CENTER in photo above), with Mrs. Laura Evans and her daughter, Rankin County, Mississippi teaching them to read, 1965.

THE PHOTO ABOVE, TAKEN in 1937, shows my great-grandmother, Louise Parker, with her grandchildren: my mother, Armelia Leonard, and my uncle, Horace Leonard.

CHAPTER 8

DAVID STREET AND EMMA PACKARD

EVERY MORNING I GET up and remember my Native American Ancestors, and I remember my African Ancestors. I remember that hidden underneath all of this concrete we walk on, are unmarked graves. It is my goal, no, my responsibility, to give them all the respect they deserve through living my life to its fullest, through "being something." They and other determined souls like them, are my motivation and source of strength.

My maternal great grandmother, Louise Street Parker born June 12, 1884 in Holly Springs (Valley Park) Mississippi, told me that she never saw her father, (or Poppa as she always called him) David Street, sleep! He always sat on his porch in Mississippi with his shotgun, guarding his precious children. Poppa was Cherokee and born in 1800. He never knew his parents and was forced to work on the plantations in Richmond, Virginia, during the days of the inhuman system we know as slavery. He was taken, kidnapped as a child; we can only imagine what happened to his parents, siblings, family, and community. I imagine they were killed in one of the too-numerous-to-count wars against the Native Americans. Such pain, loss, fear, and insecurity can carry on for generations. There is not a day that I do not think of the system we call slavery and its history. And I am determined not to let the victim take the rap.

Poppa may have been present on the plantation, he may have worked by force for free but he was never really a slave. How could he have been a slave and still produced a son as bold as Uncle Sol, a daughter as forceful, outspoken and determined as my great grandmother? I frequently make the simple analogy of a thief stealing a woman's purse. Who is the criminal, who should take the rap? Certainly not the victim!

A powerful man of short stature, Poppa wore a single braid down his back, and he befriended other Native Americans in his predicament while being a comfortable and full participant in the African American experience. Poppa was a wise man who knew the stars and predicted the weather; he was a farmer and a good father who never forgot his ancestry. He suffered the sale of his first wife and children. (Can you even begin to try to imagine the "sale" of your loved ones? What kind of twisted mind-set could justify the selling of human beings?) He remarried, had more children and when that wife died in 1897 after the Civil War, or "Peace Declared" as my great grandmother frequently referred to it), took on the responsibility to raise his children alone. My great grandfather was a single parent in 1897.

He had great hopes to own some of the land that was his already, so after "Peace Declared" he moved the family from Virginia to Mississippi. Which at that time was thought to be a land of promise! He pooled his money with two other men and they collectively bought a piece of land. None of them could read and the lawyer, who prepared the papers for them, forged them and had the land signed over to himself! It's a story that was re-told many times by my great grandmother and it still stings today. There was no recourse for such travesties to justice in those days.

So he went on with his life, but he never forgot; and he continued to tell the story to his children, hoping that one of them would find life kinder than he did. He raised his children, farmed and lived to be one hundred and five! With even the highlights of his life being so dramatic, I guess I understand why he never slept.

My paternal great grandmother, Emma Packard, never knew her origins; never knew her parents; and was never sure of her ethnicity. She was ninety-eight when she died in the 1950s in Chicago. She was a tall six-foot woman, born in Little Rock, Arkansas and was an orphan. She was a casualty of her times but she commanded a quiet kind of respect. She looked Native American and African perhaps, but we will never know. She was married to my great grandfather Aaron Packard who was perhaps of West African or Congolese parentage; he was a short, melanin-rich man. She had no say-so in the marriage, he just "chose her" to be his wife, as my dad tells the story, and the people who "took care of her" were glad to see her go. One less mouth to feed I suppose.

I remember my great grandmother, although she was quite an old woman when I was a child. I am so grateful that she passed my way. She was deeply religious, quiet, and always seemed to see more than she would tell. She is famous in my dad's mind because of her psychic prediction that came during a dream. As I remember my dad telling the story, she called him and warned him to avoid a certain park that was in their Southside Chicago neighborhood. She had seen him being attacked by robbers and being killed in the assault. My father heeded her warnings, but about a few days later his uncle, Art Brown, died in a robbery attempt in the same park and in the same manner she had described! She had all the details correct, except the person.

Even though Uncle Art was seriously wounded he put the thief in a hammerlock and dragged him home a half a block away where neighbors called the police who came and arrested him. Uncle Art was still alive when the paramedics arrived, but died at the hospital; he had always vowed to never let a thief take his hard-earned money and he kept his word!

My dad was very close to his grandmother, she had helped to raise him when his parents divorced while he was a toddler. So those events remain stunning for him. One of Grandmother's daughters, Aunt Willie, earned her living as a psychic. Of the many stories I hear about Aunt Willie's exploits, everyone always agrees that she was a "darn good psychic." Dad says that not only was Grandma

Packard psychic but she was also a herbalist and only went to the doctor once towards the end of her life for a dental problem! So in the spirit of the old African adage we say "You are not dead until you are forgotten." Grandmother Packard and Grandfather David Street will live forever!

NO MORE WAR (CHANT)

The essential message that Dr. Martin Luther King and his mentor Mohandas K. Gandhi left for us was one of living a life of non-violence. As a young fiery civil rights worker I could not accept such a concept. I only agreed to it as a tactic, as an essential part of our training. But as the old folks used to say, "just live awhile." I've lived long enough to see that no matter what the cause, violence only begets more violence. This poem, written right before the start of the wars that immediately followed the attacks on the Twin Towers on September 11, 2001, is written for all mothers. I have given birth to five children and I know what it takes to bring life to this planet. I don't ever want to see mine or any mother's child injured or killed in war. So this poem stands as a mother's mandate and pledge for peace... Peace is Possible.

No more War
Mothers of the World
No more War
Mothers of the World
We must take back our children
And teach them the truth

War begets more war

Mothers of the World

No More War (Chant)

No more War

Mothers of the World

fear and pain
and hurt
and sorrow,
that's what war is

listen my children listen
War is people blown apart
the smell of flesh and steel
that is what war is

No more War
Mothers of the World
No more War
Mothers of the World
we must take back our children
and teach them the truth
War begets more war
Mothers of the World
No more War
Mothers of the World

War is Pain
War is bloodletting

War is babies disfigured

War is insane

War is hurt

War is trouble

War is War

No more War

Mothers of the World

No more War

Mothers of the World

we must take back our children

and teach them the truth

War is broken bones

And mangled flesh

War is seeing your son's decapitated body

War is the continuous nightmare of it all

pain beyond relief

War is the screams in the night of unprotected women

War is cold

War is hunger

War is unrelenting

War is no peace

War is your home capsizing on top of you

War is smothering

No More War (Chant)

War is fear

War is despair

War is tears, and crying and lamenting

War is anticipating the bombs overhead

War has no shelter

War has no peace

No more War

Mothers of the World

No more War

Mothers of the World

we must take back our children

and teach them the truth

War carries with it a great guilt

War rewards criminals and punishes the faithful

It silences the music

Retards creativity and high ordered thinking

War dehumanizes

War is dog eat dog

War brings out the worst in human beings

War increases hatred

War incites revenge

War is War

No more War
Mothers of the World

No more War
Mothers of the World
We must take back our children
and teach them the truth

War begets more war
Mothers of the World
No more War
Mothers of the World
No more War
Mothers of the World
We must take back our children
And teach them the truth

WAR BEGETS MORE WAR

GRANDFATHER

In 1978, when the three traditional governments of the North American Indians, specifically the Dine (called by the Spanish "Navajo"), the Lakota (known to the English speaking people as "Sioux") and the Haudenosaunee (called by the French "Iroquois") sent out a radio appeal for the African-American community in Washington, DC to meet them in Malcolm X Park, my whole family (myself, my husband and two children) went. Some had come all the way from Alcatraz Island off the coast of San Francisco! We spent the entire weekend with them in that historic park. They had come to petition President Jimmy Carter to honor the treaty agreements made between them and the U.S. Government and requested our support. Watching proud, traditionally dressed Native People come into that park and meet, face to face with the African American community, many dressed in colorful African-inspired fashions, was as stunningly dramatic as it was historic. We communed, played music, ate, talked and we were given the poem below with the instruction to recite and share it as often and with as many people as we could. It became part of the Xaba duo repertoire with Baba Ndikho playing drum and singing haunting Native American chants and me reciting the poetry. I have to always prepare for this poem because the spirits of many people always come through and it can become a physically taxing experience, making it difficult to maintain my composure. Read and listen to the voice of your Native American Ancestors and pledge to do your part in righting the wrongs . . .

Grandfather, Great Spirit,

You are the Ultimate Power, who created the universe, and all life within.

Grandfather, to many spirits you have given life on this earth and to each you instructed on how to live according to your ways.

As I come from the womb of my Mother, the Earth, you gave me life. You have given me the choice of two ways to live

The good way and the bad way.

And you have given me a sacred pipe with which to learn from my relatives, the winged, the two-legged, the four-legged and those that live in the waters, to walk the good road, which is red.

Grandfather, as I stand before you today, forgive me if I am weak. Today we ask for your mercy.

Grandfather, you have created the Red Man, the Yellow Man, the Black Man, and the White Man. To each you have given a domain and a purpose. Today as the Red stand before the Yellow, the Black and the White, we pray that you may touch their hearts so that they may understand our purpose.

Grandfather, today we remember the countless members of our Red nation who have sacrificed their lives so that we, the coming generations may live to see this day.

Grandfather, today we remember the slaughtered millions of Buffalo, Elk, Deer, Eagle and all the rest of natural life that you have created and have given purpose.

Grandfather, today we remember our Grandmother, the Earth, who gave us birth and who continues to nurture us, her children.

Forgive us if we become weak to allow her exploitation and continued destruction

Grandfather, today we pray for the coming generations.

Grandfather, today we pray for all the living

Grandfather, as one Spirit, one Body and one Voice we send this prayer.

Grandfather, hear us today for there may not be a tomorrow for us,

—*The Red Man*

CHAPTER 9

THE CITY OF MAGIC

IN 1970 I FOUND San Francisco to be a city of magic. Built on seven hills and sitting right on the edge of the Pacific Ocean, this alone makes it a legendary place to inspire creative thought. So it was in this magical environment that I met and married South African keyboardist and loyal ANC (African National Congress) member, Ndikho Xaba. We had two pianos in the house. One in my three-year-old daughter, Genhi's, room and one in the living room used for the daily rehearsals that gave birth to the band "The Natives." The music that they produced was as political as it was intense. Baba Ndikho held daily South African history lessons for the band members and their families, and is the only artist I know of who regularly did South African war chants and battle (Zulu vs. English) reenactments musically on stage. He was determined to use music to free South Africa from apartheid's evil grip and the members of the band

and their families, all children of the duplicity of America, were determined to help. The band was like family. I cooked so we could all eat vegetarian cuisine after rehearsal, my young daughter, loved by all, served as our lucky charm and attended every rehearsal and performance. The musicians played their hearts out, making every attempt to understand this concept, that music can create powerful, meaningful, lasting change. During the sets, I started writing poetry to the music, as did some of the other fans. It was during these intensely political and creative times that the concept for writing a book was born. Here is one of the poems I wrote during those times:

FOR OUR CHILDREN

A child sits
and waits for her turn
to skip rope
I see she is a princess
a future queen
I see a beautiful human being
whose beauty surpasses
all these words

You are flowing
gracious

regal

you are

black

elegant

moving to the rhythms of the earth

you are

in harmony to earth's

song

you are

song

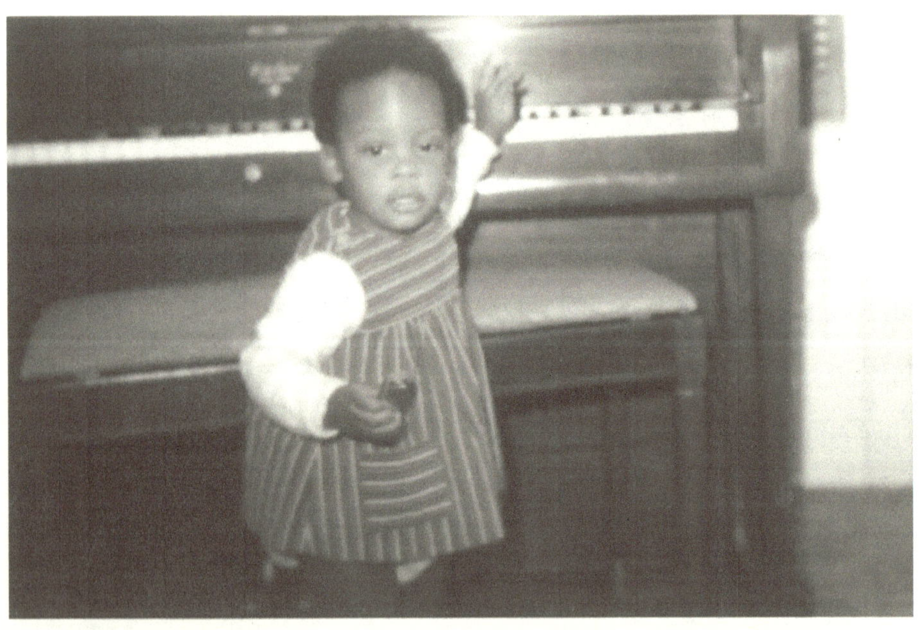

MY DAUGHTER, GENHI, THE band's "lucky charm," with her harmonica and playing her dad's piano, San Francisco, 1970

As time went by and we left San Francisco, I continued writing poetry. The Natives disbanded but the sense of family and connectedness remains. The Natives morphed into The Xaba Duo and I took my place on stage reciting poetry and playing percussion. We were supported by many fine musicians in every town we lived in. Every atrocity that we heard about on the streets of Soweto or Guguletu or Lesotho or anywhere else in Southern Africa was met with a new poem, with piano accompaniment and a powerful fiery delivery. We wanted people to come out of their comfort zones, look again at the atrocities being committed in Southern Africa in their names. For our loyal audiences, our performances were spell binding and life changing.

The destruction of thousands of homes, thousands of dreams in Crossroads, Cape Town, South Africa did not miss our attention.

When press reports read something like this: "On September 14, 1978, South African police raided a settlement known as the Crossroads, a squatters' camp near Cape Town, South Africa," my response was to write poetry. Crossroads was a community of 20,000, where black people had constructed a small city complete with two schools and a system of local government. Although most of the residents of Crossroads had lived in this area for over a decade, and ninety-four percent of the family heads held jobs in Cape Town, to white South Africans these people were *illegal residents.* Two adults and one infant were killed in the confusion as the police fired tear gas and bullets into the crowd. After the attack, the government announced its intention to level the houses of corrugated iron. These were once homes for the now displaced thousands... Responding to reports like this one, I wrote poems like the following, which I recited to piano, drums and other instruments many, many times...

WHEN I START TO TALK

When I start to talk
I start to sing
and when I start to sing
I start to cry

but I must stop
there is no time for tears
no time to grieve
for the struggle continues to continue

and when I start to talk
I must listen to what I am saying
and when I sing
I must know what to sing about
for the tears must move me to actions
actions designed to win

my enemies try to force my hand

but I must guide my emotions
into well-conceived
revolutionary actions
actions designed to win

my children are in jails and I am so far away in another jail…
my actions must be designed to win

my brother has passed in a foreign land
and there is barely time

to bury him
let alone grieve
my actions must be designed to win

and there are husbands
separated from wives…
my grief knows no bounds
and yet, I must not cry
my actions must be designed to win
To the Enemies of the Sun we say
"We will gather at your door in such number that the rumbling of our feet will make the earth tremble."

and when I start to talk
I start to sing
and when I start to sing

I start to cry...

but I must stop, there is no time for tears...

no time to grieve

for my actions must be designed to win...

I realized the poignancy of these words years later when I was in Tanzania teaching at the ANC school, Somafco, as I watched ANC comrades burying our dead and literally no one cried, as we sang and read poetry continuously through the burial process, until the last shovel of dirt covered the casket and we "passed the spear." It was an amazing, life-changing experience.

HAPPY TO BE NAPPY

"Say it Loud I'm Black and I'm Proud" *was the refrain heard throughout the country in the late sixties; a refrain made famous by the popular singer, James Brown, and proud we were. Looking through pictures of Miss Black America 1970, I saw nothing but what were popularly called Afros or Naturals (as they were originally called). Not a chemical head among the group! Natural black hair, kinky hair, curly hair, nappy hair, for some of us it was not a style but a statement of being, a reaffirmation of self; a recognition that "God don't make no junk!" Here's a poem in celebration of Nappy Hair.*

Happy to be Nappy
The beauty is in the curl
the twist
the loop
the hug close to the head
the intertwining of the locks
and black so black

like wire
like lambs wool
like cotton and black so very black
the beauty is in the black

PHOTO ABOVE SHOWS SOME of our black and proud fans in the park in San Francisco for The Natives' last performance there in 1971.

YOU CANNOT HOLD US BACK

For we are *change*
fresh as a morning dew
and new as a baby's laughter
and no you cannot
hold us back

neither pronouncements nor
mandates
declarations nor laws,
no you cannot
hold us back

we are the heart beat of the universe
we are the pulse of creation
we are the ray of light that shines for the lost ones
we are the burning spear and
the cool evening breeze
we are hope
and the fierce winds of stormy rain
we are life
and you cannot hold us back

we will never be daunted

our heads will always be high
we do not know fear
discouragement is something
we do not understand
from difficulties, set-backs
delays hardships,
we will build a bridge
to the endless future

we will step forward
we will move on
we will create a new day

we are *change*

we are *change*

we are *change*

fresh as a morning dew
and new as a baby's laughter
and no you cannot
hold us back...

WALKING THE EXTRA MILE

When all roads have been blocked
When all peaceful actions have failed
When the rain continues to flow
When there is nowhere to duck
When the fire rages in your eyes
And you cease to sleep
When you are
Up against the wall

Then you will know
Who you are...
All else will cease to matter

When all around you
You feel uncertainty
And when the cold winds—they blow
When prayers go un-answered

Then you will know
Who you are
And the power of song...

CHAPTER 10

BECOMING CADRES OF THE ANC

THE ANC (AFRICAN NATIONAL Congress) is now South Africa's governing party, but it began as a liberation movement with its founding roots going all the way back to 1912. As such, it was the oldest liberation movement on the continent of Africa. The power and respect that this historic organization has enjoyed is awesome, defying comparison to any other organization I had ever known. My husband was a loyal member of the ANC Youth League before he was forced out of the country and into exile for his political activities. We were a liberation household, teaching our children South African history alongside African-American history. Our heroes were the great Pan-Africanists of the day and of days gone by. We were reverent to our combined histories and to our heroic ancestors who had sacrificed so much on our behalf. Xaba means to spread out and we did our share of moving so much so that none of our five children were born in the same place!

In 1980 my family was living in New York, where the ANC had Johnny Makhatini as a permanent delegate to the United Nations (UN). He is now deceased, but I remember him as a skilled diplomat, with the ability to relate to heads of state and ordinary citizens with ease and respect. He was a listener, and a passionate man. People felt comfortable and at ease in his presence. It was under his leadership that a meeting was called for all American-born wives of South African ANC men. There was an air of anticipation on the part of the wives as we gathered that Saturday afternoon in the sparsely furnished ANC office that sat blocks from the UN. For sure, we wives were supporters of the ANC, but no one could figure out why the ANC officials would want to meet with us. The air of seriousness seemed mystifying and baffling to us. Finally, the secrecy was broken as we were briefed on the reason for this historic meeting. We were honored when we were described as women of influence and intelligence who had great political organizing skills. But that didn't answer the question as to why we were sitting in the ANC office. They went on further to say that the movement did not need us to sit on the sidelines any longer. Our organizing skills were needed to work whole-heartedly on behalf of the ANC. We were told we were entering a new phase in the fight against apartheid and we must now bring this struggle to every corner of the globe. So, unanimously, unceremoniously, in one fell swoop, we all became cadres of the ANC. We had walked into that small office as supporters of the ANC and walked out as members! We were honored, of course, but wondered what was really expected of us. Very soon after that historic meeting, we organized Saturday meetings for our children to learn South African history, culture, freedom songs, dance, etc. The children were very excited to be an integral part of the freedom struggle and quickly learned songs and formed a performing group. They were truly ambassadors for freedom and became quite a hit performing regularly for various events sponsored by the UN. They were a full part of the propaganda tool to bring an end to apartheid.

Feeling a deeper sense of purpose and belonging in the new South Africa that we would help to build, inspired me to write poetry about the daily brutalities that were taking place inside the country. These poems were written to be performed and my husband and I continued our piano/poetry duo. We were the Xaba Duo, passionate, idealistic, artistically vibrant, and politically relevant. What follows is a poem from those days. We expanded the duo concept to include many talented, hard working musicians, all of whom shared our passion for South Africa's liberation. We did countless benefits, seminars and fundraisers for the ANC. We believed we could make magic with this music of ours... and we did!

LEFT TO RIGHT: OUR children, Makhosi, Genhi and Maqhawe at Rockcreek Park, Washington, DC in 1980. The family was leaving DC on our way to New York.

WE ARE MAGIC

We will create sunshine out of tears
Hope out of despair
Life out of death traps
Flowers will grow on barren land
We Are Magic

We will create light out of darkness
An oasis in the desert
We will make a way out of no way
We Are Magic

We will make music out of the wind
We will dance when there is no song
We Are Magic

We will create sunshine out of tears
Hope out of despair
Life out of death traps
We will work and never get tired
We will create bright moments
Out of a sea of darkness
We Are Magic

CHAPTER 11

SOLOMON MAHLANGU FREEDOM COLLEGE

IN SOUTHEASTERN TANZANIA, IN a valley surrounded by the breathtaking Uluguru Mountains, there was a large parcel of land. This long abandoned, German built sisal plantation, is called Mazimbu. It was on this land, gifted to the ANC by the Tanzanian government, that the ANC built the Solomon Mahlangu Freedom College (SOMAFCO).

Somafco was founded abruptly, shortly after the 1976 student uprising in South Africa. On June 16, 1976, students protesting against the proposed threat of being taught in Afrikaans instead of the usual English, staged a school walk-out. They and the world were shocked when many of them were shot dead by the then-infamous South African regime. This was the beginning of the Soweto uprising.

With the children under intense daily physical attack, many ran away, some were shipped out of the country by their parents, told that they were going on holiday, only to end up at the ANC offices in Lusaka and later in Tanzania. Through skillful diplomacy by the ANC, negotiations went into high gear with the Tanzanian government to begin Somafco. With the help of the international community, the ANC started to build a school, beginning with a high school. Soon a primary school and later a nursery school and crèche for babies were added.

The Xaba family responded to Somafco's urgent call for teachers, preferably South Africans, by applying to teach at Somafco. And like a dream come true, we were eagerly, with the recommendation of the ANC Toronto based Chief Representative Yusuf Saloojee, accepted.

Our family arrived in Mazimbu in June, 1983, after having been given a memorable send-off by both the Native American and ANC community in Toronto. At our final going-away performance, one South African female comrade cautioned me not to work so hard. I had no idea what she was talking about... I would soon find out...

We were delighted to be rewarded with the honor of serving at Somafco, and the physical beauty of the place was breathtaking. I never tired of looking at those majestic mountains hidden by the most unusual cloud formations I have ever seen. At Somafco, I was at times a primary school teacher, crèche "director" (I always said the crèche directed itself!), and as an administrative aide in the high school principal's office. Visiting African Americans touring our facilities were always impressed that I was in the administration. My modest reminders that looks were deceiving and that I had no policymaking functions fell on deaf ears. In their minds, one of their own had made it to a very prestigious, coveted position in the anti-apartheid movement; she had "done good," and they were proud. I didn't want to dampen their pride, so I smiled and thanked them instead rather than giving them lengthy explanations.

Somafco was a mini South Africa with an overpopulation of young people. (Sometimes the young people would let us know it too by throwing all night parties with speakers that blasted throughout the complex. They loved Marvin Gaye! We adults suffered through it; after all it was one of their few sources of entertainment.) These were very urban kids thrust into an extremely unfamiliar rural environment in a foreign country, away from family, and going to a school that had intense academic expectations. They were refugee kids, with a twist. They were being groomed to take over the new South Africa and make the promises of the Freedom Charter come true. *Everyone* there had a story of torture, abuse, dreams deferred. Many had been to jail and it was common for people not to use their given name, but to use pseudo names in case the spies among us would report it back the South African authorities.

We once encountered a young man who had been tortured by the South African police while in custody for political activities. He was released with the understanding that he would come to Mazimbu and put poison in the food of our students who were fed in four large communal kitchens. His conscience got the best of him and instead he turned himself and the lethal poison over to the ANC authorities and was not punished; they understood his plight and got him out of the complex. He could have wreaked havoc on our small community of two thousand.

Once when funds became scarce the administration talked about cutting out the newspapers that were our life source to events in Southern Africa...but the people all had a swift unified response, "We would rather go without food than go without news!" Needless to say the papers stayed! These were real politicians, revolutionaries determined to bring change to war-torn South Africa.

WITH MY EYES WIDE OPEN

With my eyes wide open
I saw the angel of death

I watched wide-eyed in horror
As he went from house to house
searching for a vulnerable one
to take with him

Maybe if I sat very still
He might ignore me...

It was bedtime
I had laid down,
closed my eyes
I suddenly felt very sick
hot and cold at the same time
What was going on?
What were these images that looked like dreams with my eyes closed...
I sat straight up in bed
...and real figures with them open
I couldn't be dreaming
Could I?

Fighting to gain control of my mind

To block out these hideous images
Made it all worse
I had just lain down
I wasn't even asleep
How could I be dreaming?
I fought harder
But I was helpless
I was in a wild state of hallucination
I had to close my eyes
The hallucination was too vivid
I was too scared
But when I closed my eyes,
It was even worse
I felt trapped in my own body
the harder I tried to free myself
the worse it became

Now I understood
I had malaria!
I had seen others with malaria
Their eyes wide open

Hallucinating

Screaming

Sometimes needing to be restrained

as they tried to run away from themselves

I never understood

Until now

Whenever I got a clear second

I tried to focus on what to do

I had to get out of this

I prayed a desperate prayer

To regain my mind

Very, very slowly I found myself
walking down
the long hallway
to my kitchen...
being lead by ancestral forces
they just kept instructing me
to do as I was told
don't try to analyze
or question
or otherwise figure out what was happening
That could come later
"Just do as you are told," they said
"And you will live to tell the story"

I released my need to be in control
As I was lead to the kitchen
Lead to fresh hot African pepper
and some *pau d'arco* herb that
a kind friend had given me
before I left the states for Tanzania

I obeyed
as I was instructed to boil water
Cut up the pepper
Add the *pau d'arco* to the pepper
pour the water on top
and wait to let it steep
I was moving in slow motion
At times my spirit seemed
to move out of my body
Watching me

This all seemed painfully slow
And the hallucinations continued through the whole ordeal
I was hot and cold at the same time
I ignored it all and did as I was told.

As soon as it cooled I started taking small sips
This allowed me to make the slow trek back to my bedroom
It seemed to take hours

I BEAT IT!

Finally in my bedroom I continued slowly to sip more and more of the remedy. I was gaining in strength and clarity, determined not to go down to malaria. The hot and cold feeling finally turned to hot and the hallucinations began to dissipate, they were more sporadic... I seemed to have more control over my thoughts... finally I broke out into a sweat and I knew I had won! I began to laugh out loud saying, "I beat it, I beat it!"

My husband came in after his usual night out with the boys at the local "bar." One look at me sobered him up! Confused with my actions, he asked if *I* had been drinking? As the sun started to rise, I just kept laughing saying no, no, I had beat it... I had beat malaria!

Many people came to me when they noticed that neither my children nor I were getting sick with malaria and I told them about the remedy; trying to remember all the ancestors had told me. Many people listened and it helped them to prevent or lessen the effects of the malaria. My two younger children and I took the remedy every day, and neither they nor I ever got malaria again. My husband reasoned that since he ate hot pepper every day cut up in his food he didn't need to take the remedy. I tried to convey what the ancestors had indicated to me as best I could remember that the healing was in the oil of the pepper, it needed to be released with hot water... it just wasn't the same as eating it in food...

CHAPTER 12

THERE'S NO ESCAPE

I **REMEMBER TALL GREEN ELEPHANT** grass and a bird that perched itself on top of it. The bird was so light that the grass never moved. It always seemed like a miracle to see a bird. So light, so light, she could perch herself on top of grass and it would never move . . . never once move . . . and when I wanted to let go of some of the tension I felt from teaching full time, managing a household, counseling students, participating in the political life of the complex, and performing poetry, then I walked way to the top of the hill. I wanted to be like that bird, high above everything, watching but undisturbed.

On my walk I came across an anthill as tall as me! And way up here in nobody's land I was very surprised to find an isolated family living on that side of the hill, all alone in such a desolate place.

Then, as I walked further, *they* came, suddenly, quickly, in an instant. I began to respond. I danced, you know that dance called the stomp? I asked for forgiveness for having stepped on this, the home of the red army ants. They attacked hard and fast and in multitude. There was no time to do anything but dance, stomp, and run before they bit me to death!

I made it through shaken, but essentially okay, deciding it was better to just live with the tension and forget this escape stuff!

CHAPTER 13

TANZANIAN WOMEN

THE WOMEN IN TANZANIA are among the most beautiful in the world, with beautiful smooth chocolate brown skin, I don't ever remember seeing anyone with acne! Whenever I got the chance to go to Morogoro town, fifteen miles away, I was always impressed by the beautiful array of colors the women wore. The town seemed to be a whirlwind of yellow, red and orange. The national dress is a kanga (tied skirt) and a shawl of the same cloth. The shawl would be worn in a variety of ways depending on region, religion, and personal preference. Here is a poem to honor both my beautiful Tanzanian and South African sisters (the last stanza about the black shawl refers to the South African women).

THE SHAWL

And she WORE the shawl
It was rectangular
Yellow, red and orange
Draped across both shoulders
Open in the back
Then gently TOSSED across the right shoulder

And SHE wore the shawl
It was rectangular
Yellow, red and orange
draped over her right shoulder
Then under the arm of the left
Then draped over the right shoulder

And she wore the *shawl*
ever so gracefully
draped over both shoulders
opening in the back

Her shawl was worn over her head
Then tucked behind her ears
As it fell loosely down over her shoulders
While she tossed the left piece ever so gently over her right shoulder

And She?

Well, she embraced her newborn child *with her shawl*

Bending over balancing the little one carefully on her back

She placed the middle of the shawl at the middle of the baby's back

Then tucked the shawl neatly under the baby's feet

As she tied the open piece above her breast

And her shawl

was black

and triangular

For she was symbolic of the ceremonial mourning

The passing over of yet another comrade

She was symbolic of woman

The observer

Her quiet mournful presence was necessary to complete the ceremony

Her shawl was symbolic of status

Her spiritual wealth in the community

She was Mamkhulu—the great mother

Indlovukazi—the woman elephant queen

All that she knew or would ever know

Was wrapped up in her shawl, sometimes red

matching her graceful headpiece

The shawl triangular

Was always tied in front

“HE’S NOT HEAVY, HE’S my brother.” In the photo above, taken in Evanston, Illinois, in 1990, my son Sipho carries his younger brother Dingane on his back, the way he saw Tanzanian women and men carry their young ones.

CHAPTER 14

THE HIJACKER

YES, I TRIED TO hijack the ANC ambulance. Yes, I stretched the truth and told the ambulance driver that my semi-comatose, presumed cerebral malaria-ridden husband was being released from the Morogoro hospital today. What I didn't say was that I was signing him out of the hospital and taking him home to care for him, myself! Yes, I was crazed by the many days of my husband's semi-comatose state, the endless daily tests that never came up positive for *anything*, including the malaria for which he was being treated. I was crazed by the gracious but inadequate facilities of the Morogoro Hospital, and the endless bureaucracy of the ANC medical staff. So when a sympathetic friend of mine told me about a wonder drug called Fansidar that had been known to bring malaria patients out of a comatose condition overnight, and that she had a contact to get some... and then she sort of off-handedly said, "You might as well bring him home," in that instant I decided to do it! So here I was with the results of that split decision and there was no turning back. The ambulance driver sensed my state of being but played along with me. I got in the ambulance and he engaged me in light but pertinent conversation... "I didn't know Baba Ndikho was out of the coma, I just saw him yesterday," commented the ambulance driver. "Oh, he's making a great recovery," I lied. "You know that hospital is so crowded, he'll do better at home with me and some help from the clinic staff." "Does Mrs. Maseko (the head nurse at the ANC clinic) know about this?" he asked. "Oh, yes," I replied (another lie). He seemed to believe me, but it was difficult to tell, he was the kind of guy who just did his job. His job for now was to drive the ambulance back and forth from Mazimbu to Morogoro, taking patients, picking up patients and bringing food to the sick. South Africans would rather starve than eat hospital food. So we brought food to our patients every day. I was desperate, trying to make light conversation and pretend to be normal. If he just got me back to Mazimbu, I'd be home free!

He said he would take food to the other patients and wait for me outside, since no other patients were scheduled to come home today.

I went in and asked to see the head nurse. When she was summoned I told her I was here to take my husband home. With no questions asked, she said "Okay, I'll give you these papers to sign." As I signed the papers she looked at me sympathetically, knowing I was crazy. She took him off the IV and the catheter then turned to look at me. I said I would go outside and get the ambulance driver, and could we have a few male nurses to lift him on to the cot. She agreed. I went outside. No ambulance, no driver... I walked to the road to see if I could see him... I looked both ways... no ambulance, no driver. As I said the ambulance driver was a man who did his job. He took people back and forth to the hospital every day. And if someone was being released, he was given his or her name. He had not been given Baba Ndikho's name; his was a big case. The community was baffled, the doctors were baffled. No one had ever stayed in a coma this long and lived. If Baba Ndikho was coming home it would have been big news. He would have been told... I had only fooled myself... I stood there in Morogoro town, a small dusty East African town of about 50,000 people feeling... helpless.

How could the driver just leave me (Easily, it was leave you or lose his job!) For the first time in my life, I doubted my commitment to being a freedom fighter, a cultural worker, a message bearer. Had I spent all my life dedicated to the struggle to be abandoned in my time of need? The movement had abandoned me. It was one of my lowest points... I had failed in my mission, failed my family, my husband lay helpless in the hospital, and I was all alone—or so I thought.

It was turning dusk and I knew there would be no more ANC cars coming to the hospital tonight. I couldn't walk to the nearest ANC house, it was too far and I wasn't sure of the directions. Besides, in East Africa, dusk means dark in five minutes. I couldn't stay in the hospital. I walked back and forth for a while and just sat down on a big boulder as it turned dark.

After what seemed like a lifetime, I saw the sweetest thing: Headlights! I was not all alone! The ambulance! Surely they would be humane, see it my way, and allow me to take him home. They all rushed out of the ambulance, ran over to me and demanded to know what I thought I was doing. I got the usual speech from Mrs. Maseko about how we South Africans were guests in the country of Tanzania and how we must do nothing to upset the Tanzanian government. After all they were almost the last African country to host refugees (Mkimbizi or runaways as we were spitefully called by the Tanzanians) and we had to be *gracious*, accepting whatever help they could give us and then supplementing that help as tactfully as we could. We didn't want to insult them or highlight their obvious lacks. Everyone knew that I was going through a difficult time, but was this any way to act towards a country that has so *graciously* hosted us, the liberation movement? My actions were jeopardizing all of the ANC.

When I got a chance to talk, I reminded them that for all I knew my husband was dying in there, no one expected for him to live, no one had ever lived that long in that kind of condition. He was being written up in the medical journals as an unusual case. We were up against the wall. He couldn't fight for himself, so I had no choice but to fight for him. They couldn't take care of him, he had gotten bedsores, the hospital was overcrowded, and the hospital ran out of drugs all the time. I had to go and get the drugs from the ANC clinic, take it to the hospital and watch the Tanzanian hospital staff put it into the IV. The Tanzanian hospital staff resented that. But the ANC officials would only give me enough drugs for one day and insisted that I stand and watch as the drug was put into the IV (drugs were hard to get and rumor had it that some of the hospital staff would take whatever the ANC gave them and sell it on the black market) What kind of solidarity was that, with everybody suspicious and angry with one another? I knew I could take care of him. The Tanzanian staff could care less whether he was in or out of the hospital. They had enough problems of their own. Anyway it would give them another bed for patients who desperately needed it. All I needed was the ambulance to take him home! They challenged my ability to take care of him, asked what medicines I would use? I couldn't tell them about the Fansidar without implicating my friend. We went on and on like that and got pretty loud.

TIME OUT!

My friend, who had originally suggested I take him home, was also an ANC official, and she was with this group. She took me to the side to try and work though a compromise. She said to me that she realized that she had been the one to suggest the Fansidar and yes, she had said, "you might as well take him home." But after further thought, she realized she didn't really mean that. She apologized for putting such a thought in my head. Surely we could find a way to work this out. She went over and talked to the group.

Finally, we were all brought back together in that hospital parking lot. “Look,” Mrs. Maseko said, trying to be as conciliatory as her fiery authoritative persona allowed her to be, “Nomsa, we know you have been through a lot. Conditions are quite poor here in East Africa and we know the strain you have been under coming to the hospital every day and still raising your three children. We realize we have not been as supportive as we could have been. We know you are from the States where you are used to better conditions; you have no extended family here and this has been quite shocking to you. So if you will accept our apologies (I knew I was being set up now!) We would like to offer you a compromise. Give up your fight, sign him back into the hospital, have his IV and catheter put back in and *tomorrow*, we will find a better, more private wing of the hospital. We will even send our staff over every day to attend to him.”

I neither trusted nor believed her and quickly reminded her that I had asked that he be put into the “private” wing of the hospital weeks ago, and was told that the waiting list for it was weeks long. Even the “private” wing of the hospital still had drug shortages, bedsores were a problem, the screens were broken and mosquitoes still got in. It was the same hospital, just two in a room instead of thirty. If the ANC was willing to do private duty in the Morogoro Hospital, why couldn’t they do it in Mazimbu where we lived, especially since at this point we were providing all the drugs? In the end, I couldn’t play politics with my husband’s life. I cried, they looked sad, my friend seemed as if she was torn between what seemed to make common sense and her responsibilities as an ANC official. She had to let a friend down in order to do her job. The hospital staff seemed to have monitored this loud conference in their normally quiet parking lot. But they never batted an eye when I went back in and signed him back into the hospital. They put him back on the IV and catheter, and he was unaware that all this drama was taking place. We all drove home in the ambulance in cold silence. I cried a little more as I contemplated Plan B.

THE NIGHTMARE BEGINS

Now that I had refused their conciliatory offers I was treated overnight as an enemy of the state. Ambulance drivers and other ANC personnel were ordered not to take me to the hospital; I was under a ban. So I had to get rides from local Tanzanians who were not affected by ANC policy. Some ANC drivers would drive around until they were sure no one was watching and then let me in. At dusk I would wait in town at the appointed place for rides; ANC vehicles would pass me by. I would cry a few silent tears.

After dark I would go to the ANC house across the street from the appointed place. They were wonderful. I was so emotionally and physically drained by it all. But they would sit outside and flag down unsuspecting ANC vehicles to take me back; I never knew how they could do it in the dark. Their house was in a dark spot and since it was night and no one could see that it was me, drivers deemed it safe. Some expressed their outrage at the ban, others said nothing, but all were sympathetic. All remembered Chico, who died right before Baba

Ndikho got sick. He was a talented, lighthearted guitar player and a dedicated cadre of the ANC. He was a friend and used to rehearse with us in the house. He was paralyzed by a tractor accident and was supposed to be taken to Germany for treatment, as the local hospital was not equipped to do the kind of surgery he needed to regain use of his legs. He was never taken. He got severe bedsores. He died from those bedsores, but not before he cursed the people responsible for not attending to his needs. He had no wife, no family. No one wanted to see a repeat of that sad, seemingly unnecessary scenario, so people commended me for my fight. I was grateful but numbed by it all.

WAKE UP!

One day I came to the hospital and Baba Ndikho was talking to a comrade who was new to East Africa and didn't know his story. I was amazed! They both looked at me and wondered what all the excitement was about. I started to tell them that this man had been in a coma for a month. Not talking, not moving beneath his waist. Not recognizing most people, even his own children. Most people had given him up for dead. In fact the rumor spread all the way to the States that he had passed away.

I always believed he would make it. He always did things unexpectedly, I reasoned, so if he were to die, he would have done it suddenly, not lingering like this. What a joy! What a blessing! I just let the conversation drift into ordinary, insignificant events... what a luxury.

BED SORES

My mother had been a nurse's aide when I was a child, but I had no first hand knowledge of bedsores. I was aware that Baba Ndikho had them, but he was always bandaged when I came. I always checked to see that there were fresh bandages every day when I visited and I was totally unprepared for that day, a few days after his great awakening... there we were, several of my friends and I circling Baba Ndikho's bed when... one of the bandages partially fell off and we saw the most awful site of infected flesh, covered by scabs with pus oozing out.

I was traumatized; we were all traumatized. Mrs. Maseko happened to be there, visiting another patient. We hadn't spoken since that eventful night and my ban. But I rushed over to her to tell her of this most awful sight. We must do something, I begged; please, we must get him out of here! She went over took off the entire bandage, it was much worse than I imagined! I nearly fainted. But her words were even more of a shock than those pus filled sores, she started her usual speech about the *graciousness* of the Tanzanian government and how we were guests in their country and we should be careful not to offend them by taking our patients out of their hospitals. If we started taking our patients out of their hospitals, they would stop taking our patients and then where would we be? She got about two sentences into her speech when I snapped! All I remember is screaming and running, some of my Tanzanian friends tried to ask me what was wrong; but I was paralyzed and could only scream and run. Some kind soul caught me before I got to the street and restrained me. The rest was a blur, someone put me in a car and someone drove me home in silence.

ARETHA FRANKLIN AND JOHNNY WALKER RED

I'm not normally a drinker and have been known to be a good parent. But I didn't pick up the children that night. There was a white South African couple who had twins who acted as permanent babysitters for me every day as I went to the hospital to visit my chronically ailing husband. They finally couldn't take the stress of my two little ones and their twin boys, especially after the ban, since it took me several more hours to get home. It gets dark in Tanzania every night at 6 p.m. and many nights I got home after 8 p.m. School started at 7:00 a.m. and everybody was either a teacher or a matron and went to bed early. This was the struggle and we all worked hard. So I was not offended when the wife said she was exhausted and asked would I please get someone else. Who? Everyone else was overworked too.

So every day I would ask a different person to watch my children. Many nights I would come home and my children would be outside, with no apparent adult supervision... the night of my great hysteria fortunately they were safely with the matron across the road from me. I didn't go to get them. Instead I walked over to Unit 3 immediately after I was dropped off. And I was not surprised that all my friends who had circled the hospital bed with me were already there. They already had the top off the Johnny Walker Red, had the music on and were expecting me. We all knew why we were there, to forget what we had just seen.

When I came in we made a pact that no matter what tomorrow would bring, tonight we would not mention Baba Ndikho or the horrible sight we had all witnessed. *Tonight we must just forget.* We drank, we told jokes, we sang. One brother kept telling me how he liked my American accent, I sounded just like Aretha Franklin, so we put on all the Aretha Franklin records we could find and I sang as much like Aretha Franklin as I could. I drank and drank but never got drunk, but when I thought I might be able to sleep without seeing that horrible sight, it was time to go home and get the kids.

TIME TO RETREAT

I stopped going to the hospital for a while. I started receiving messages that Baba Ndikho was asking for me. Mrs. Maseko said that the hospital was doing their best to get the bedsores under control, but they needed my help. Now that Baba Ndikho was awake, he wanted to move and had to be restrained. I told her I thought he should be brought home; it was because of the intense heat of East Africa, their neglect, overcrowding, and genuine disbelief that he would live that he was in that shape. I didn't know what more to do. Everyone seemed to have a different point of view. I seemed to have no control. In effect, I told her it was because of her that he was still there, so she should deal with it.

But I was praying, being quiet, and preparing to bring him home by "any means necessary." We were the talk of town. People were beginning to take sides; a revolt was brewing. The word went out on the underground grapevine that I was preparing to bring him home and needed trustworthy allies. Some people agreed to bring me bandages, some tape, some towels—whatever we had. I spoke clandestinely with an ANC doctor who was visiting from Angola. He was skilled in treating war wounds and if I agreed to his anonymity he would gladly treat the bedsores at home and train me how to care for them. He was sure we could do this, and wondered why all of this was such a big issue. He assured me that he had dealt with war casualties in Angola and that he was prepared and qualified to deal with this. Everything was in place, I started to feel like something between Harriet Tubman and Malcolm X… I was looking for a sign…

LOOKING FOR A SIGN

After three days I went to the hospital. No Baba Ndikho. When I inquired, they told me he had been falling out of the bed; so they decided that, in his best interest, he should be put at the back of the ward, *on the floor*. He was there all right, confused, complaining, writhing around, trying to figure out how he got in this mess and how he would get out. He was happy to see me but confused that it had taken me so long. No matter, I had my sign. I told him to quiet down, take it easy, I was in control, and we were going home.

GOING HOME!

The ANC ambulance guys were at the hospital. I loudly went up to them and asked if they would take us home now under these most extreme circumstances. I was purposely making a scene and made an impromptu speech about injustices perpetrated against the masses, sounded like something I had said in street rallies in Chicago! They declined. I said fine, I was hiring a local ambulance and would take him home on my own. Would they help to pick him up or were they too cowardly to assist their own country person in his time of need? Did they need someone to tell them what was right? The lines were drawn. I had shamed them, split their ranks. They were unsure; some said yes, others backed off. One of my friends bravely stepped forward and offered to pay for the ambulance. The hospital wanted to get me out of there quickly, as people were beginning to gather. I was possessed with the God of Courage, which many years later I was to learn is called *Herukhuti* by the ancients.

We were quite a scene in that rented ambulance, me, Baba Ndikho, and my brave friend. And with the ANC ambulance following directly behind us, we sort of looked like a parade. Baba Ndikho had come out of the coma, but his memory was slowly making a comeback. So in the ambulance, I was filling him in on who he was. While he was still in the coma but semi–awake enough to talk to respond to questions, I had asked him if he knew his name...he'd shaken his head no. So I'd told him his name, I'd told him his parents' names and where he was born. That was enough at that time. Now as we were in the middle of this drama, on our defiant trip home, he asked me, where was home? I almost cried as I did when I had to tell him his name a few weeks before, and explained to him as best I could the situation; being careful not to give him too many overwhelming details. I told him he had three children who would be waiting for him and explained that I was his wife. As we got within a few kilometers of the complex, the ANC ambulance, which had been following meekly behind us, made an abrupt takeover and led us into the complex! You could have heard a pin drop in the complex... it seemed as if no one was outside but everyone was peeking from their windows. Baba Ndikho was back, it was a victory for people's power! We got in okay, got him settled, but before I could call the doctor to attend to the bandages, and eat, there was a knock on the door. All of the ANC officials from the complex were there, the principal of the high school, primary school, nursery school, party officials, there were eleven of them, some of them my dear friends, even my brave friend who had paid for and rode home in the ambulance with us. The cream of the ANC hierarchy in East Africa were *all* in my living room.

"BUT I WAS COOL..."

So what did I do, with that stunning assemblage of power? I did like Oscar Brown taught me... "I was cool," and acted as though this was a normal occurrence on a Saturday afternoon. *So Ms. Cool sitting there, barely enough space for you to sit in your own living room, folks had to get chairs from the dining room, what are you going to do now...what are you going to do now?* All I could do was listen. Obviously they had a single message and they wanted me to hear them clearly. I waited, and listened, and breathed. They started with the Maseko attack dogs. Mrs. Maseko was the head of the clinic. Mr. Maseko was the principal of the high school. He is the only man I have ever known to have given a negative eulogy at someone's funeral; he was a "my way or the highway kind of person," and so was his wife. So when they started out I knew we wouldn't go much further than their point of view. What kind of people would deny transportation to a wife trying to visit her husband in the hospital, what kind of people would deliver scathing attacks on a young person at their own funeral? Opinions aside, they were my leaders and I had to listen, this was important. And listen I did, as they tried to court me, woo me to their point of view. How well they understood what I was going through, how awful to have a spouse so ill in a foreign country, etc., etc. And I had no medical training, no medicine, how could I expect to pull this off? *I couldn't tell them of the ANC doctor who was just waiting to come and clean the wounds. It would implicate him.* Then came the patriotic stuff; however, in the interests of the liberation movement and because of other people who would get sick after this, they couldn't let me keep him at home. Other people might get the idea that they could do the same and then we would have chaos; maybe the Tanzanian government might decide that we were ungrateful visitors; maybe the Tanzania government might kick us all out! I didn't want to be a threat to national security, did I? I waited, let them all speak. Some of them were my friends, who some hours earlier, were on the "bandage brigade." But at this moment of truth, they went with the group. If I thought their arguments were plausible, I would have agreed. But my mother had taught me better, "the squeaky wheel gets oiled." And letting a family member (or anyone, for that matter) die on the floor of the mosquito-ridden, overcrowded Morogoro hospital was not acceptable. Neither was playing politics with his life to get a better deal. I told them so and reminded them of Chico. Feeling a keen sense of betrayal I looked at all of my friends and said individually to them, "And you too, you agree with this?" They all said... yes.

I am Tanzanian, I am as Tanzanian as I am South African, I am as South African as I am African born in America. Identity is not just born by birthplace but also by understanding. I was understanding the ANC leadership very clearly.

As a final futile gesture I reminded them of my rights as his wife. The ANC leadership made it very clear to me that this was the struggle. And under these extreme wartime conditions, *I had no rights.* My husband was a cadre of the ANC and I was a cadre of the ANC and we were bound by its rules. They had tried to talk to me kindly but they had made the decision that it was in the best interests of the ANC for him to return to the hospital. They would provide care twice a day at the Morogoro hospital, coming to change his bandages, bringing him food, etc. My mind was screaming, *Why are you driving fifteen miles away to provide a service you could perform right here?* But I said nothing, there was nothing more to say. The ambulance was on its way...

GOING BACK

Immediately after they left, one of my friends, a volunteer from Holland who was organizing the "bandage brigade," slipped into the side door. She wished me the best and said she had done all she could but the ambulance was pulling up outside and she had to split! I asked her if she thought they would force my hand if I staged a sit-in on Baba Ndikho's bed. She said they had sent army guys, big army guys and mumbled "yes" as she quickly exited...

They came. I put up a valiant, if weak, bedside sit-in. They just looked at me and said "Sis' Musa, please don't force our hand." I was clearly outnumbered, so I backed off and back to the hospital he went.

The rest is kind of a blur. Mrs. Maseko took over, twice a day going with a team to clean all the infection out of the three huge "stick your fist inside of" bedsores. They did a magnificent job keeping them clean, I was impressed but still dismayed at all of this seemingly wasted energy coming and going. I was now welcome in the ambulance and even encouraged to go. From outcast to honored guest! My, the wonders of the struggle! I had to take a back seat but watched carefully as the trained nurses attended to the sores with precision every day, several times a day. I was learning a lot.

But, this honeymoon was short lived. Baba Ndikho had diarrhea one day and everyone said I must have given him some herbs or something to cause it. I tried to defend myself; I had given him nothing but food. No one believed me! All the ANC staff was angry with me, all the hospital staff was angry with me. I was ordered not to bring any food to the hospital and not to touch the patient! If I refused, I would be banned from the hospital! I was not allowed to bring bags into the hospital and was watched carefully whenever I came. "This too, shall pass," I reminded myself. By this time I had developed a great relationship with ancestors Baba John Coltrane and Dr. W.E.B. Du Bois. I kept their biographies open on either side of my dresser and read from them every day, and while I am not Christian, I was amazed at how powerful the Twenty-Third Psalm is. I was certainly in the "valley of the shadow of death… " These prayer rituals sustained and strengthened me. I stayed in a state of grace and began to watch the events of our lives unfold.

Baba Ndikho was eventually transferred to a more private wing of the hospital. But those conditions were still quite unacceptable. After a few days there, he begged me to get him out! I tried one more time going to "friendly" ANC officials. They agreed to look at my case again; but before that could happen Baba Ndikho checked himself out of the hospital, got his own ambulance and showed up at home!

Mrs. Maseko was quite angry. By this time some calmer officials were beginning to see that this was starting to look like a personal vendetta. They tried to talk to her and say, let's just let it go. He's getting stronger, just treat him at home, it's easier, cheaper, etc. With this intervention, we lasted a week or two, she sent nurses every day;

they trained me well. I was grateful but waiting for the other shoe to fall. And fall it did. Without our consent, she arranged for him to be transferred to Dar es Salaam to have an operation, a skin graft that she said would help to heal the bed sores quicker; she seemed weary of this slow process. Dar es Salaam was a five-hour drive away. I wouldn't be able to go. He would be all alone. We didn't know what condition the hospital was in, and no one could quite explain the details of the operation except to say it involved skin graft. So when we refused to sign the papers, we were back on the "shit list" again. Overnight the nurses stopped coming, I was denied bandages (my friends with the "bandage patrol" got busy). I had paid close attention to the nurses and knew how to do it and got a few of my friends to help. So I thought okay, we can do this...until I went to the commissar to pick up my monthly stipend and they denied me money. We had been given an extra stipend every month to buy vitamins, fruit and high protein foods so that Baba Ndikho could heal; food was his medicine. That extra money meant a lot, but obviously in her anger Mrs. Maseko had stopped that. So hysteria set in and there I was again crying on a dusty Tanzanian road this time with my children, whom I tried so hard to shield from life's realities, looking on saying "What's wrong, Mommy? Why are you crying?"

THE PEN IS MIGHTIER THAN THE SWORD

While I had no real answer I could verbalize to my young boys, I went home, pulled out my old trusty typewriter that my parents had bought me when I was twelve years old and typed a fiery, if frustrated letter to the "officials." I challenged their sense of conscience, fairness, and their ideals. It was just a way to get steam off. I didn't expect an answer. To my surprise I got an immediate response, an apology even! The money was reinstated and I was asked to come the next day to pick it up! What a difference a day makes!

The patient finally recovered, although deeply scarred. And you would think that after such a trying experience we would have become a stronger couple, but that was not our case...

TRY TO FORGET

About some things
we won't write eloquent poems

About some things
we will not talk

About some things
no songs will be sung

Some things we will just try to forget
just try not to remember
just hope that they will be
washed away by the tears we couldn't cry

CHAPTER 15

ONE AND A HALF MILLION DOLLARS

AFTER MY HUSBAND'S BOUT with malaria I took a "patient" into our home. David, (his pseudonym), was wanted by the South African police for non-political crimes. He was a real rarity. I don't know of any other person in Mazimbu who was wanted for anything but so-called political crimes against the state.

David was quite a character, a master storyteller. He was a slight man maybe weighing a hundred pounds after a shower, who had befriended my husband while they were both patients at the Morogoro hospital by literally giving him the shirt off his back when my husband was cold late one night. It was such a touching scenario; I promised him if I could ever do anything to help him, I would. Africa is very family dependent. People expect your family to assist you in times of need, and in our complex, if people didn't have blood family, they grouped up according to language, city and/or township.

Most people found a family group or groups to fit into, but as in all social groupings some people fell through the cracks. David was one of those.

So when David showed up at my door, newly released from the hospital, TB free, and needing a home, I felt more than obliged. I didn't expect the favor to be him living with me, but a promise is a promise. None of the adults in our house were too thrilled about this. They reminded me that they had not been previously consulted; besides, I had small children who would be put at risk if there was still some TB left. I assured them that we had a big living room and we could put up a curtain to block off a living space and he could have his own separate space, and he would be tested for TB every month. If the disease returned they would hospitalize him immediately. He was now part of my family, I reminded them. They gave in, David stayed.

These days I earn my living as a storyteller and my audiences always ask me where I get my stories from; the answer is always "I listen to my elders." David is one of those elders that I listened to. His remarkable life had turned him into a master storyteller that we all listened to, spellbound and in awe, night after night. Sometimes I had to put the children to bed knowing they were too young for some of David's exploits. Over and over again he told of his life of crime, he was an expert thief. He and his gang would break into large pharmaceutical warehouses at night and steal drugs that they would then sell on the street market, making huge profits. He was a bold, arrogant, highly organized leader of his illegal organization and also a devoted family man (kind of reminded me of the Mafia stories I had heard in Chicago, ruthless thugs who still went to church on Sunday!) who built a beautiful house for his wife and all of his family members. They were all living well on his huge bank account.

He recounted a story of how they broke into a warehouse one night and he brought a six-pack along to share with the "boys." They were frightened and wanted to get out as soon as possible but David assured them he was in charge of this and told them to relax and have a beer! They reluctantly followed his lead and that story of bold folly followed him everywhere he went.

Well, after awhile his wife sensed that his "good luck" was about to run out and she repeatedly begged him to stop the thievery and go into a legitimate business. They didn't really need the money anymore. He made a pact with his wife that after one last heist he would "retire."

Since this was to be his last burglary he wanted to make it his best. And it was! They managed to get in and out of a pharmaceutical warehouse with 1.5 million in drugs; no time for beer this time. It must have been the talk of the underworld! But somewhere, someone became a turncoat and tipped off the police. He was arrested at his home and "interrogated" by the police. They knew this was a big operation and they had caught the "kingfish." But there were more people involved, and the police were anxious to put an end to the havoc this gang was wreaking and break them up. David pretended to break under interrogation and gave them some names he made up, but all the while he was planning his escape.

So...as David tells the story, after roughing him up, the police handcuffed him, put him in the back of an ordinary looking police car and drove him around Soweto ordering him to point out the house of one of his fictitious high-ranking gang members. Clever David saw this as his only opportunity to escape and so he led them up and down hills, around corners, through alleys, all the while trying to loosen up the handcuffs. Even though the cuffs were tight, his slight build worked to his advantage and he managed to break free while pretending to be cuffed. That was the moment when he "remembered" the house of his crony. The police were excited, thinking that they finally had a catch. Being told by David to go to the back door, *they left him alone* in the car as they staked out the house. There were tall bushes around the house so they didn't see him as he made his escape.

Jumping over bushes, around corners, in and out of the neighborhood he knew so well, apparently he had just enough time (a few minutes) to escape, and knowing time was working against him, he begged some woman to take him in. He always seemed so obliged to that woman whose name he never knew.

They combed the neighborhood looking for him. She hid him for a few hours until night. The story always got vague here, but he got out of the country that night, maybe to Swaziland, maybe Botswana. But during this period he had an epiphany and pledged himself never to go back to the life of crime. He had such deep regrets about not heeding his wife's pleas. He had dreams of getting his wife and children out of South Africa, but that never happened. The police kept a tight watch on his house, his wife, and everyone associated with him. He got bits and pieces of information but could never resume direct contact.

Eventually he became politicized and decided he should do something positive with his life. He made it to Lusaka, Zambia, to the headquarters of the exiled ANC office, and after some convincing was allowed to join the ANC. He eventually became a trusted driver for the ANC leadership, and always claimed he had made a huge donation to the movement from a secret account he gave them access to. While the reformation of his life was real and he stopped stealing and became quite a political stalwart, he continued to drink and smoke heavily and eventually contracted TB. When I met David he was on his fifth battle with TB!

My youngest son at the time, Sipho, was two years old, and slight of build as well. So David took him under his wing and became his special uncle. It seemed to us that crying was Sipho's hobby, he cried for long periods of time, for reasons we could never fathom and no one seemed to be able to stop him, no one except David. Right in the middle of a crying spell David would look at him sternly and in a deep, loud voice say "Sipho, why are you crying? Are you a *man* or a *mouse?*" And through his tears Sipho had no choice but to stop crying and reply "I'm a *man*, Uncle."

CHAPTER 16

FORTY DOLLARS AND THREE KIDS

DESPITE ALL MY PERSONAL and political troubles in East Africa during the three years I spent there, I loved the land and its people dearly and promised all my Tanzanian friends that I would return someday, and I will keep that promise.

By April of 1986, my U.S. family knew that the three children and I were scheduled to return soon, but the phones in Mazimbu were on again, off again, and I never had the opportunity to give them a final itinerary. We spent a few days in Dar es Salaam at a beautiful resort type place run by the Salvation Army. It was actually a school for disabled children and they had small cabins that they rented out to pay for the school. This was another scenically beautiful place, with lots of land, a baseball field, and a swimming pool. It was quite touching to watch and interact with disabled kids, some of them without limbs, as they swam and played baseball. It made my own problems seem quite small.

The phones had been out in Mazimbu before I left so I thought I would call my folks from the ANC office in Dar, but transportation was an issue and I never made it to the office. My husband had insisted on going to Dar es Salaam to see us off. I was uncomfortable with that, since I knew he was having a difficult time with our leaving. I was on watch. He remained sober for most of the time, but on the last day, the day that we were leaving, he started drinking and showed serious signs of strain. So when we finally got to the spot at the Dar airport that was designated *for ticketed passengers only,* without incident, I sighed a big sigh of relief!

Traveling from Dar es Salaam to France through Saudi Arabia, I heard and saw such well dressed, well spoken Africans. I was truly proud and impressed but had never heard the languages I was hearing now. While I enjoyed the flight and the fact that we had made it without a last-minute incident, my mind was consumed with the fact that here I was with forty dollars and three kids, on my way to Chicago and no one knew I was coming! When we got to France I got an airport phone and called my Aunt Gwen. Her number had been changed and she had an unlisted number! I called the French operator and explained my now-desperate situation. I was traveling from Africa with children, I had not been able to contact my family directly and no one knew that I was coming! Surely this woman could help, I reasoned in my mind. She was unhelpful, downright rude as she told me my aunt had an unpublished number and that she could not give it to me. Perhaps in my desperation I had not made myself clear, so I tried to be clear, and told her that I knew she had a job to do and could not give me her number. But could she please call U.S. information and have them call my aunt and tell her I was coming and give her a number to call me. She refused.

I stared at the phone; I really couldn't believe she could refuse. But she did, she refused and hung up on me! I went to the airline people and explained my story, by this time our plane was boarding and here I was with forty dollars and three kids (almost felt like being barefoot and pregnant) going to Chicago from France and no one knew I was coming. I quickly gave the airline attendant my aunt's name and now defunct phone number and asked if she would get a message to my family. She promised me she would do her best.

Previously I had asked to be put far from the smoking section of the plane because the smoke aggravated my allergies. So for this leg of the journey, the very nice airline people gave me and my three kids seats in first class! Talk about a blessing! By this time the two youngest children were wild with the excitement of the trip and couldn't sit still for even a moment. They were playing with the seat controls or turning the radio and TV sets on and off constantly, clearly out of control and getting worse. My teenaged son and I were both getting weary, so I looked at him and said, "You take one and I'll take the other and we'll just hold their arms and legs until they go to sleep." And that's what we did. In five minutes they were sound asleep. If we had tried that strategy in coach they might have arrested us for abuse! Ah, the joys of the privacy of two seats across in first class.

I weighed my options regarding what I would do once I got to Chicago. I was sure (almost) that the Chicago telephone operators would call my family. Or maybe there was a travelers' aide or maybe I would just wander around the airport until my forty dollars ran out. I decided to get some much needed rest, enjoy the comforts of first class and notice how big the Atlantic Ocean really was...

The landing in Chicago was so smooth, like a feather touching the ground. We were all whisked away on a shuttle bus to the airport when my name was called on the loudspeaker and I was told to report to a certain desk as soon as I got to the terminal. There I was told they had my aunt on the phone. What a reunion we had by phone. That airline attendant in France had kept her word. She called U.S. information and they in turn called my aunt. To celebrate, I bought the kids ice cream cones with the forty dollars and even had change left over!

WATER OF WATERS

Water of Waters
River of Life
Unending cycles
what message do you have for me, this time

Water of Waters
River of life
Moving through me, this time

Water of Waters
River of life
one drop upon the stone
rush
towards the great un-ending
source

Water of Waters
River of Life
what are your secrets
what story for me, this time

Water of Waters

Water of Waters

River of Live

Unending cycles

what message do you have for me, this time

CHAPTER 17

LEARNING TO DRIVE

HE WANTED TO LEAVE in December, but no self-respecting woman with two children to raise, would allow herself to be left by her spouse in the middle of a Wisconsin winter! So I insisted he wait until June. And so on June 1, 1999 my husband left with a one-way ticket for his home country of South Africa. *Meantime, the stick shift Honda that I had bought from my aunt sat in the garage.* He kissed me goodbye, reached for the roll of duct tape (just in case) and left with a friend of ours taking him to the airport. He was gone, our twenty-eight year marriage was gone too. *Meantime the Honda that he had driven because I couldn't, sat in the garage.*

I had family pictures taken before he left and we did one last performance together at an artsy club in town. We had performed together all those years in the U.S., Canada and East Africa as the Xaba Duo, he was the master keyboardist and I the poet /percussionist. All our adult offspring came to this final performance of the Xaba Duo and several performed. It was a vibrant, energetic politically-charged performance, typical of our style. We treated it like a celebration and it was. My husband had been a political exile from his country for thirty-four years; it was clearly time for him to return home. Our marriage was rocky at best.

In 1989 my husband had left Tanzania and joined us in Chicago and we tried our best to reconcile our differences, but we had too many obstacles in our way. I was clear that this was the end of this chapter.

My spouse, on the other hand, was a dreamer. Somehow without money, without a plan, with idealism, we would make it work. *Meantime, the car sat in the garage.* I had two kids still in school, and a teaching job to get to. I clearly needed to drive the car. I had spent months doing serious meditations, visualizing myself driving, replacing all my fears of driving with truisms/mantras. I went to driving school, friends came by and gave me a few lessons. It all helped, every effort was part of the process. *But meantime* ... there's a certain special something that comes up when you hit the wall, when your options are limited. It's called "quit making excuses, just do it."

So I drove that '84 Honda stick shift that my aunt sold me, in and out of the garage, around the block, around two blocks, only between 10:00 a.m. and 2:00 p.m., never in rush hour and only on side streets. I only drove if there was absolute silence in the car, no talk, no radio. I have been known to pull the car over and threaten to evict children from the car for talking too loud or for talking at all!

Finally I was driving on big streets, then on highways. Driving out to the country, driving to Madison, to Minneapolis and the crown jewel, driving to Chicago! I drove back from Tennessee once, straight to Chicago in twelve hours. I was so proud of myself. It's hard for us to remember the days when I couldn't drive. I dared to make the journey in uncharted waters and I was rewarded with sweet, sweet victory.

PICTURE OF AUTHOR DANCING with the children at her birthday celebration in Chicago in 1996.

KEEPER OF THE SACRED DRUM

Deep in the heart of the earth, she is
Keeper of the sacred drum
Away from all
Yet all with one
Keeper of the sacred drum, she is
Playing the drum
Silently playing the drum
The heartbeat of the Universe
Keeper of the sacred drum, she is

Message bearer
healer
teacher
repairer she is

Keeper of the sacred drum, she is

SAWUBONA[4]

I see

I see in you

The god that I am

I see

I see in you

the god that I am

I *am* the god in you

that I see

I see

the god in you

that I am

I am

I am the god in you that I see

I see

I see in you

the god that I see

that I am

I am

I am the god in you

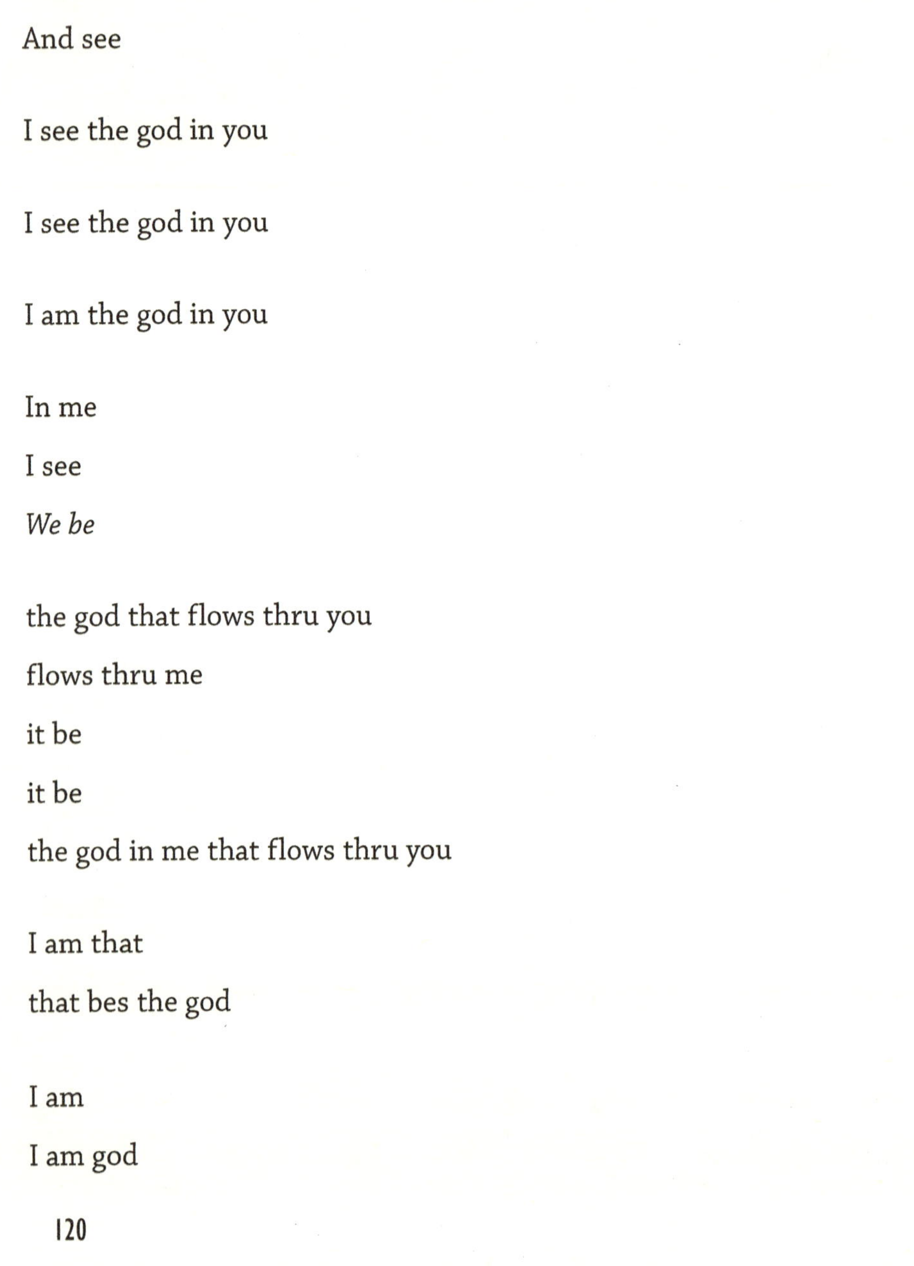

that I see
And see and see
And am
And am
And am
And see

I see the god in you

I see the god in you

I am the god in you

In me
I see
We be

the god that flows thru you
flows thru me
it be
it be
the god in me that flows thru you

I am that
that bes the god

I am
I am god

It flows thru you and flows thru me and

We be God

4. Zulu greeting that means “I see the God in you.”

IT'S BEEN A LONG TIME COMING... (CHANT)

It's been a long time coming...
but my change is come

It's been a long time coming
but my change is come

it's been a long time coming
it's been a long time coming
it's been a long time coming
but my change is come

it's been a long time coming
but my change is come

it's been a long time coming
but my change is come

it's been a long time coming
it's been a long time coming
it's been a long time coming
but *MY CHANGE IS COME*

www.ingramcontent.com/pod-product-compliance
Lightning Source LLC
LaVergne TN
LVHW091004080826
845145LV00003B/1123

* 9 7 8 0 6 1 5 3 0 7 3 0 5 *